INTRODUCTION

On its very first deployment, the Navy's newest aircraft flew combat missions in support of Operation Enduring Freedom. An F/A-18E from VFA-115 is positioned for launch on Catapult 4 aboard USS ABRAHAM LINCOLN, CVN-72, for a mission over Afghanistan on October 5, 2002. Before LINCOLN returned to her home port, VFA-115 would also fly missions as part of the air campaign of Operation Iraqi Freedom. (U. S. Navy)

Less than one-third of the squadrons that are scheduled to fly the Navy's newest combat aircraft have begun their transition to the F/A-18E and F/A-18F, yet the Super Hornet has already flown numerous combat missions over Afghanistan and Iraq in support of Operations Enduring Freedom, Southern Watch, and Iraqi Freedom. VFA-115, the first operational fleet squadron to transition to the Super Hornet, engaged in combat from USS ABRAHAM LINCOLN, CVN-72, during its first cruise with the F/A-18E. Beginning in October 2002, they attacked Taliban and al Quaida targets in Afghanistan, then they moved to the Persian Gulf to fly missions in southern Iraq as part of Operation Southern Watch, enforcing the no-fly zones in that region as coalition forces were increased in preparation to remove Saddam Hussein from power.

As LINCOLN heading home, she was turned around and sent back to the Persian Gulf as war with Iraq became more and more certain. Along with other aircraft of Carrier Air Wing Fourteen, VFA-115's F/A-18Es flew combat missions during Operation Iraqi Freedom beginning with the very first night of the war. The squadron was soon joined by VFA-14 and VFA-41 aboard USS NIMITZ, CVN-68. These three Super Hornet squadrons played an important part in the successful completion of Operation Iraqi Freedom while proving the capabilities of the aircraft.

Writing a book about an aircraft that is still early in its operational life has unusual challenges. There are no file photos nor records in museums or other archives. There are not a lot of squadrons that an author can visit to conduct interviews, obtain reference material, or take photographs. Instead, he must rely on the assistance of the aircraft's man-ufacturer, the military, and the few squadrons already operational with the aircraft.

In preparing this book on the Super Hornet, The Boeing Company generously provided several dozen photographs of early EMD and LRIP Super Hornets that were used for tests and evaluations. Photographs of developmental details and photographs of Super Hornets assigned to VX-9 and VFA-122 were also provided. These were essential in illustrating the early years of development which began in 1995 and continued until 2001. The U. S. Navy provided photographs of the Super Hornet's participation in Operation Enduring Freedom and Operation Iraqi Freedom.

To obtain the scores of detailed photographs required in a Detail & Scale Series publication, a trip was made to NAS Lemoore, California. VFA-14 and VFA-41 provided invaluable assistance in taking photographs of both the F/A-18E's and F/A-18F's details. Over eight hundred photographs were taken in the cockpits, under the radome, in the equipment bays, in the cannon bay, and all over the entire exterior of both Super Hornet versions. Live AIM-9M and AIM-120 AMRAAM missiles were photographed after they were loaded on aircraft for a firing exercise. This book would not have been possible without the superb cooperation of these two squadrons.

As this book is written, new scale model kits of the Super Hornet are being released, and others have recently been announced. The Modelers Section at the end of the book covers the existing kits and gives a brief preview of the 1/48th scale Super Hornet models that have been announced by Revell-Monogram.

The F/A-18E and F/A-18F will continue to replace Tomcats and older versions of the Hornet in Navy squadrons for many years to come, and important upgrades will be added. Another version, the EA-18G Growler, is scheduled to become operational with the fleet in 2009. But the Super Hornet has already written important chapters in its operational history as it extends the Navy's striking power in America's war on terror. This is the first publication dedicated exclusively to the Super Hornet and it provides a very detailed and close-up look at this new combat aircraft.

WHY THE SUPER HORNET?

The first four versions of the Hornet were considered to be versatile aircraft, but they were always criticized for having insufficient range. This meant that two or three external fuel tanks had to be carried even when aerial refueling was available. This left only two stations to carry weapons that could be used against ground targets. This F/A-18C from VFA-131 heads toward targets in Afghanistan with a GBU-16 Laser Guided Bomb (LGB) under its left wing and a GBU-32 Joint Direct Attack Munition (JDAM) under its right wing. The other pylons capable of carrying air-to-ground munitions are taken up with three external fuel tanks. (U. S. Navy)

By the end of the 1980s, F/A-18A and F/A-18C Hornets had replaced the A-7 Corsair II in all but a few Navy light attack squadrons. By the time Operation Desert Storm took place in 1991, only one A-7E squadron remained to participate in the war. Former A-7 pilots praised the speed and agility of their new Hornets which also had far better air-to-air capabilities than the Corsair. They enjoyed training for both air-to-air and ground attack missions. The Hornet's service in both peacetime and in combat was quite successful, and it proved to be a very versatile aircraft. However, there were two areas in which the Hornet was soundly and justifiably criticized. First, the range of the aircraft was very limited, and tanker support was almost always a requirement. Second, the capability to carry external stores was considerably less than the A-7 it had replaced. These two shortcomings caused some critics to complain that the Hornet couldn't go anywhere and couldn't do anything when it got there. While this criticism may have been overly severe, there can be no argument that the range and ordnance shortcomings were indeed problems of a considerable magnitude.

The two deficiencies also worked against each other. The lack of range could be offset to some degree by carrying more than one external fuel tank, but the tanks caused more drag, and worse, they took up pylons that were needed to carry external stores. So carrying two or three external fuel tanks meant that fewer bombs or missiles could be loaded to attack ground targets. Hornets often flew to their targets carrying three external fuel tanks and only two weapons under their wings and fuselage. An increased weapons load meant

that less external fuel could be carried, and the weapons added weight and drag, which further shortened the range that could be flown on internal fuel and only one external fuel tank.

This trade-off between carrying external fuel and external ordnance is a consideration on all fighter and attack aircraft, but it was critical with the Hornet. As the Navy approached the retirement of the A-6E Intruder in the mid-1990s, the A-12 Avenger II, originally scheduled to replace the Intruder, had already been cancelled. As a result, the Navy faced a much diminished attack capability.

To correct this problem, several alternatives were considered. One was to produce new F-14D Tomcats which would have an added precision ground attack capability. Existing Tomcats would also have this capability added. But after only a few new F-14Ds were produced, the production line to build more new F-14Ds was closed. While existing Tomcats did receive a precision bombing capability, this alone would not be sufficient to provide an adequate attack capability along with the Hornet variants then in service.

McDonnell Douglas proposed a new and larger version of the Hornet with increased internal fuel capacity and more powerful but fuel efficient engines. Two additional stations were added under the wings to carry external stores, so even when external fuel tanks were carried, there would be enough stations remaining to carry a sizeable weapons load.

Both single and two-seat versions were proposed and developed, and although the aircraft were larger, heavier, and considerably different from the earlier Hornet versions, they were given the Navy designations F/A-18E and F/A-18F, continuing with the next suffix letters to indicate the new variants. But to indicate that the new aircraft were quite different and much improved when compared to the earlier Hornet versions, the Navy named them Super Hornets. As development and production of the Super Hornets continued, the F/A-18A/B/C/D versions became known as legacy Hornets. This was not an official name, but merely a way of making quick reference to the four earlier Hornet versions.

The development of the Super Hornet went very well. McDonnell Douglas became part of The Boeing Company, and the aircraft met or exceeded almost every design and performance specification. Only one major problem devel-

The Super Hornet is a larger aircraft than the legacy Hornets, and it has an increased internal fuel capacity to increase range. An additional station for external stores has been added under each wing. However, poor design planning placed the pylons too close together, and this caused problems during weapons separations tests. To correct these problems, the six wing pylons were angled outward four degrees, and the two outboard wing pylons were also canted outward 3.5 degrees. This meant that the weapons are also carried at an angle, and this increases drag and reduces range. (Boeing)

oped, and it threatened the very reason the Super Hornet was created.

During weapons certification tests, it became apparent there were some separation problems with the external stores. There was not enough space between the wing pylons, nor was there enough distance between the inboard pylons and the sides of the fuselage to insure the safe separation of the weapons from the aircraft. Unfortunately, there was not enough room under the wings to increase the spacing between the pylons. As an alternative, the wing pylons were angled outward four degrees at the leading edge. This was accomplished by pivoting each pylon around its forward mounting point, and moving the aft mounting point in toward the fuselage to obtain the four-degree angle. Further, the two outboard pylons were canted outward three and one-half degrees.

While this solution helped solved the separation problems, the angled pylons and stores increased drag on the airframe, and increased drag results in decreased range. Increasing range was the primary reason for building the

Super Hornet in the first place. With no other solution possible, the Navy has been forced to accept the angled pylons, but even with them, the Super Hornet still exceeds the range and ordnance carrying capabilities of the legacy Hornets.

When the Intruder was retired from service, the Navy also lost its primary carrier-based tanker, the KA-6D. For several years it has been forced to use aerial refueling stores on the S-3B Viking, but this has not been entirely satisfactory. The F/A-18E and F/A-18F can be configured to serve as a tanker with a D704 refueling store on the centerline station and up to four 480-gallon FPU-11 external fuel tanks under the wings. Any Super Hornet can be configured as a tanker in a very short amount of time, so they will provide the carrier air wings with a much increased tanker capability.

Another Navy aircraft that has served well past its projected operational life is the E/A-6B Prowler electronic warfare aircraft. Another version of the Super Hornet is scheduled to begin replacing the Prowler in 2009. Designated the EA-18G and named the Growler, this version of the Super Hornet will bring an increased commonality between carrier-based aircraft. This commonality will simplify logistics and maintenance requirements.

For the next decade, the Super Hornet will continue to replace older versions of the Hornet, the F-14 Tomcat, and eventually the EA-6B Prowler. As it does, it will become the Navy's primary fighter, attack aircraft, airborne tanker, electronic warfare aircraft, and, using the SHARP reconnaissance pod, it will also be the Navy's shipboard tactical reconnaissance aircraft. In performing all of these varied and important missions, the Super Hornet will rival the AD Skyraider as the most versatile carrier-based aircraft in the history of U. S. Naval Aviation.

EARLY SUPER HORNETS

With its vertical tails and rudders already attached, the rear fuselage of an early Super Hornet is carefully moved into position to be mated with the forward fuselage assembly. (Boeing)

As work continues, the wings and ailerons are added to the third F/A-18F and the sixth F/A-18E. These were the first of the two types to be built in the initial block of LRIP aircraft. (Boeing)

The first order for Super Hornets called for five F/A-18Es and two F/A-18Fs as Engineering and Manufacturing Development (EMD) aircraft. These would be used for various test and evaluation programs, and they were assigned the following Navy Bureau Numbers (BuNos):

E-1	165164
E-2	165165
E-3	165167
E-4	165168
E-5	165169
F-1	165166
F-2	165170

The seven aircraft were built before McDonnell Douglas became a part of Boeing, and the McDonnell Douglas name was at least temporarily painted on some of these aircraft.

Following the EMD aircraft, the Navy began orders for what are known as Low-Rate Initial Production (LRIP) aircraft. Early examples went to test and evaluation units and VFA-122, the squadron that would be be charged with training Naval Aviators how to fly both the F/A-18E and F/A-18F. Later aircraft began to equip the first fleet squadrons to become operational in both versions of the Super Hornet.

The first batch of LRIP aircraft included eight F/A-18Es

Work continues on the first block of LRIP Super Hornets at the Boeing plant in St. Louis. One of the aircraft in the background has already been painted. This photograph also provides a good look at the flap details. (Boeing)

After completion, each Super Hornet is flown by a Boeing test pilot to insure that everything is working properly. This flight is often made before the aircraft is even painted. F/A-18E-6, BuNo. 165533, was the first LRIP 1 F/A-18E produced in Lot XXI, Block 52. It is the same F/A-18E shown under construction in the background of the lower photograph on the previous page. (Boeing)

(BuNos 165533-165540) and four F/A-18Fs (BuNos 165541 -165544) These were designated Lot XXI, Block 52 aircraft. They were followed by an additional eight F/A-18Es (165660-165667) and twelve F/A-18Fs (165668-165679). These LRIP aircraft were in Lot XXII, Block 53.

The production rate increased for LRIP-3 aircraft with fourteen F/A-18Es (165779-165792) and sixteen F/A-18Fs (165793-165808) being completed for Fiscal Year 1999 in Lot XXIII, Block 54. Some of these F/A-18Es were assigned to VFA-115, the first fleet squadron to become operational with the Super Hornet.

Production blocks 55, 56, and 57 are the first three full production blocks and are assigned the following Bureau Numbers:

Type	Number	Bureau Numbers	Lot and Block
F/A-18E	15	165860-165874	Lot XXIV, Block 55
F/A-18F	21	165875-165895	Lot XXIV, Block 55
F/A-18E	14	165896-165909	Lot XXV, Block 56
F/A-18F	25	165910-165934	Lot XXV, Block 56
F/A-18E	29	166420-166448	Lot XXVI, Block 57
F/A-18F	19	166449-166467	Lot XXVI, Block 57

Lot XXVI, Block 58 will include thirty-three F/A-18Es and

Wearing protective clothing, Boeing workers apply the paint to an LRIP-1 F/A-18E. (Boeing)

fifteen F/A-18Fs, while Lot XXVII, Block 59 will include thirty-one F/A-18Es and seventeen F/A-18Fs. As of this writing, the Bureau Numbers for these aircraft have not been assigned by the Navy.

In addition to the squadrons already flying the Super Hornet, the Navy plans to transition seven of the eight remaining F-14 Tomcat squadrons to F/A-18Fs by the end of 2007. One F-14 squadron will transition to the F/A-18E dur-ing that same time period. Additionally, four present F/A-18C squadrons are scheduled to transition to the F/A-18Es by the end of 2007 under present plans.

With its arresting hook attached securely to a hold-back cable, E1, BuNo. 165164, goes through engine checks at night. Note that "McDonnell Douglas" is lettered at the base of the vertical tail, indicating that this photograph was taken before the company became part of Boeing. VF-142's Death's Head insignia is visible just forward of the formation light panel. (Boeing)

Above: E1 was photographed during a publicity flight with AIM-7 Sparrow air-to-air missiles loaded under its two outboard wing pylons. AGM-65 Maverick air-to-ground missiles are on the center wing pylons, and AGM-154 Joint Stand-Off Weapons (JSOW) are on the inboard wing stations. (Boeing)

Below: The second F/A-18F, BuNo 165170, makes an early test flight. EMD Super Hornets often had their type and number lettered at the top of each vertical tail, so in this case "F2" can be seen at the top of the tail. At times, the letter and number were repeated on each of the flaps and both sides of the nose. (Boeing)

TESTING THE SUPER HORNET

With an instrumentation probe on its nose, F/A-18E number 4, BuNo. 165168, makes an early test flight in a gloss white paint scheme with red-orange trim. Note that McDonnell Douglas is painted on the vertical tail, indicating that the photograph was made prior to the company's acquisition by Boeing. (Boeing)

All new aircraft must go through a series of extensive tests and evaluations to identify and correct any potential or existing problems with the design. Although the Super Hornet was a larger development of a proven airframe, it still had to go through a complete series of tests. These included a full evaluation of its flying characteristics from spin recoveries to how well it flew behind a huge tanker aircraft with various external stores. Equally as important were hard landing tests, carrier operations, and weapons certifications.

The Super Hornet did amazingly well through almost all of its tests. The one major glitch was that problems were discovered during weapons certifications. To permit it to carry more external stores than the earlier Hornet variants, the wing was enlarged and an additional weapons station was added under each wing. However, it was discovered that there was not enough distance between these stations and between the inboard pylons and the sides of the fuselage. The only practical solution that could be made to correct this problem was to angle each of the six wing pylons outward at the leading edge by four degrees and cant the outboard pylons 3.5 degrees as explained on page 5.

This solution obviously has the disadvantage of increasing drag, even when no external stores are carried on the angled pylons. When stores are added, the problem of increased drag is made worse. The increase in drag reduces range, and to some degree, this counters one of the primary reasons the Super Hornet was developed. Further, some weapons have had their fins damaged when carried at an angle through the air at high speeds.

In spite of this problem, the Super Hornet exceeds the range and stores carrying capability of the previous Hornet variants. Certainly, the goal of increasing these capabilities has been achieved albeit not to the extent it could have been had this weapons separation problem not existed.

The pilot of E4 pops the parachute as he recovers from a spin during spin recovery tests. (Boeing)

INFLIGHT REFUELING

E1, now painted in an overall gray scheme, refuels an F-14 Tomcat. (Boeing)

The Super Hornet was designed to serve as the Navy's new carrier-borne tanker using a D704 aerial refueling store on the centerline pylon. Tests were conducted to insure that the aircraft could serve satisfactorily as a tanker as well as receive fuel through the retractable refueling probe in its nose. Here E1 refuels E4 during a test flight. (Boeing)

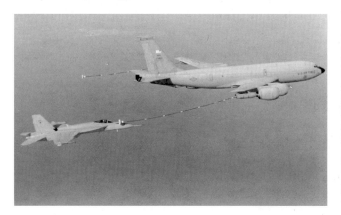

E1 refuels behind an Air Force KC-135R. Each type of aircraft handles a bit differently flying behind large tankers, so test flights are conducted to evaluate the flight characteristics under varying conditions. (Boeing)

This underside view of a Super Hornet flying an in-flight refueling test shows three FPU-11 480-gallon fuel tanks beneath the aircraft. Note how the tanks on the wings are angled outward four degrees. (Boeing)

LANDING TESTS

Above: During evaluations, Navy aircraft are put through hard landing tests to stress the landing gear and see how the plane handles during a rough landing. F1 was used for these tests, and it is shown here engaging an arresting cable while carrying an asymmetrical load of bombs. (Boeing)

Right: Another hard landing is made with only a centerline tank being carried externally. (Boeing)

Below: With a heavy load of three fuel tanks, four bombs, and two missiles, the pilot slams F1 down with the aircraft rolled to the right. This kind of test also evaluates how much ordnance the aircraft can bring back aboard a carrier if it is not expended during a mission. (Boeing)

BARRIER ENGAGEMENTS

For various emergency reasons, aircraft sometimes cannot make a normal arrested recovery aboard an aircraft carrier, so they must make a barrier engagement in the event a shore base is not close by. Each new carrier-based aircraft goes through tests to determine how it will perform during a barrier engagement. An unmanned airframe is accelerated through a barrier to see how it engages the barrier and how it is brought to a stop. These three photos show an F/A-18E airframe during barrier engagement tests. In the photo below, note that the engines, the rudders, and the horizontal tails are not installed on the aircraft. (Boeing photos)

CARRIER TRIALS

Above: One of the most important tests a carrier-based aircraft must pass is an evaluation of how it operates aboard an aircraft carrier. Launches, recoveries, refueling, deck handling, and every other aspect of carrier operations is evaluated. The Super Hornet's first round of carrier suitability tests took place aboard USS JOHN C. STENNIS, CVN-74, in January 1997. F1 maneuvers on to Catapult 4 in preparation for a launch. (Boeing)

Left: F1 inches forward under the watchful eyes of flight deck personnel for a launch from Cat 1. (Boeing)

Below left: F2 was also used in these carrier evaluations. It is shown here immediately after launch from one of the waist catapults. (Boeing)

Below right: The launch arm is attached to the catapult shuttle. Both F1 and F2 made a series of launches and recoveries over a period of several days. (Boeing)

Above: Carrying only dummy Sidewinder missiles as external stores, F1 is about to make an arrested recovery aboard USS STENNIS. (Boeing)

Below left: A second round of carrier suitability tests took place between March 3 and March 14, 1999, aboard USS HARRY S. TRUMAN, CVN-75. They were very successful and were completed three days ahead of schedule. Again, F1 and F2 flew the qualifications. With its hook extended, F1 crosses the ramp as it approaches the flight deck. Note the gray band around the nose of the aircraft that had been added since the first round of carrier trials two years earlier. (Boeing)

Right: F2 engages Cable Four as it passes TRUMAN's superstructure while making an arrested recovery. (Boeing)

WEAPONS CERTIFICATIONS

Another critical series of tests each new combat aircraft undergoes involves evaluating how weapons separate from it in flight. Each weapon must be certified for use, and they are test dropped or fired under various conditions including having different types of weapons or other stores on adjacent stations. It was during these tests that it was determined that there was not enough spacing between the wing pylons and between the inboard wing pylons and the fuselage. Here, Rockeye II cluster bomb units (CBU) are dropped from E5. A series of cameras mounted under the wing tips and under the fuselage record the drops. (Boeing)

Above: E5 is loaded with Mk 83, 1,000-pound bombs on Canted Vertical Ejector Racks (CVER) for another weapons test. The Super Hornet is certified to carry the Mk 82, 83, and 84 series of general purpose, free fall bombs with their variety of fuses and tail sections. (Boeing)

Right: Precision guided weapons have also been certified for use on the Super Hornet. A GBU-16 laser guided bomb has been loaded on Station 3 in preparation for a test drop. Note the cameras suspended from the wing tip. The numerous symbols painted on the weapon and the aircraft help measure and evaluate the angles at which the bomb falls from the aircraft. (Boeing)

Above: Every type of missile that a new aircraft will employ must also be fired from each station on which it will be carried. An AIM-120A AMRAAM is ejected then fired from one of the two fuselage cheek stations. AMRAAMs can also be carried on wing pylons, but a launch rail is required for loading them on the wing pylons. Although the Super Hornet is certified to carry the older AIM-7 Sparrow, the AIM-120 will be its primary radar-guided air-to-air missile. (Boeing)

Left: Sidewinder missiles will be the standard weapon carried on the wing tip stations. Here, an AIM-9M is fired from F2. The AIM-9M will soon be replaced by the far more capable AIM-9X. (U. S. Navy)

The AGM-88 High Speed Anti-Radiation Missile will be an important weapon in the Super Hornet's arsenal, because one of its primary missions will be the destruction of the enemy's radar systems. (U. S. Navy)

An AGM-65 Maverick is fired from a launch rail beneath the left wing of E4. Mavericks are used to attack a wide variety of surface targets such as armored vehicles on land and ships at sea. (Boeing)

F/A-18E

F/A-18E, BuNo. 165533, shown unpainted in the lower photo on page 7 during its builder's test flight, subsequently became the commander's aircraft for VX-9, one of the Navy's test and evaluation squadrons. This was the first LRIP 1 F/A-18E. (Boeing)

Generally speaking, the single-seat F/A-18E is intended to replace the Navy's F/A-18C Hornets, although this will not always be the case. The second operational fleet squadron to transition to the F/A-18E was VFA-14, which was the former F-14 Tomcat squadron, VF-14. Preliminary plans, recently released by the Navy, also indicate that at least one other Tomcat squadron will transition to the F/A-18E before the last F-14 is retired in 2007, but other Tomcat squadrons will transition to the two-seat F/A-18F.

The F/A-18E will remain the Navy's primary attack aircraft until this mission is shared with the Joint Strike Fighter (JSF) now under development. However, interviews with pilots at NAS Lemoore indicate that F/A-18E pilots spend as much time training for the air-to-air mission as their counter-

parts in F/A-18F squadrons.

The first fleet squadron to reach an Initial Operational Capability (IOC) with the F/A-18E was VFA-115. This former F/A-18C squadron reached its IOC in September 2001. In 2002, they made their first deployment aboard USS ABRAHAM LINCOLN, CVN-72, and immediately began flying combat missions over Afghanistan and later in Iraq. The second operational F/A-18E squadron was VFA-14 which deployed to Iraq aboard USS NIMITZ, CVN-68, in early 2003.

Eventually, the F/A-18Cs will be replaced by F/A-18Es in Navy squadrons, but the Marines will not receive any Super Hornets. Instead, their attack missions will be flown by F/A-18As, F/A-18Cs, F/A-18Ds, and AV-8B+ Harrier IIs until these aircraft are replaced by the Joint Strike fighter.

An F/A-18E from VFA-115 moves forward onto Catapult One aboard USS ABRAHAM LINCOLN, CVN-72, during the squadron's carrier qualifications in April 2002. Later that year, VFA-115 made the Super Hornet's first carrier deployment aboard LINCOLN. (U. S. Navy)

Above: An artist's cut-away drawing shows the location of the internal fuel tanks in the F/A-18E. Most of the interior of the center fuselage and the inboard wing sections are taken up by fuel tanks. Also note that there are tanks inside the vertical tails. The fuel jettison vents are at the top of the vertical tails just above the rudders. (Boeing)

Below: An F/A-18E from the Salty Dogs of Air Test and Evaluation Squadron Twenty-Three (VX-23) prepares to launch from Cat One aboard USS THEODORE ROOSEVELT, CVN-71. The carrier was undergoing certification of the new surface that had been applied to its flight deck when the photograph was taken. (U. S. Navy)

F/A-18E CANOPY DETAILS

Above left and right: High front and side views show the shape of the bubble windscreen and canopy used on the F/A-18E. Note that there are no forward frames on the single-piece windscreen to restrict the pilot's forward vision. (Left, Boeing; right, Kinzey)

A low view of the fully open canopy shows the seal that makes the canopy air tight to the fuselage and wind-screen when it is in the closed position. Note the rear-view mirrors at the forward end of the canopy.

The electrically operated actuator that raises and lowers the canopy is located behind the ejection seat. The upper end of the Canopy Actuation Connecting Link is connected to the Canopy Unlatch Thruster.

The inside of the canopy frame and the sill on top of the fuselage where the canopy closes are painted flat black. The clear parts of the canopy and windscreen are stretched acrylic transparencies.

At the forward lower corner on each side of the canopy rail is a small index pin. Each pin extends forward into a hole in the lower frame of the windscreen to help hold the canopy in the closed position.

Mid-way back on each side of the lower canopy rail is a small video camera. This camera, and the one on the left canopy rail, record the pilot's actions, and this can be used for review and training purposes.

The white cylinder is one of the Canopy Jettison Rocket Motors that removes the canopy in the event the pilot has to eject from the aircraft. Also note the right rear canopy latch aft of the rocket motor.

The second Canopy Jettison Rocket Motor is located on the left canopy rail. The Canopy Unlatch Thruster and Rocket Motor Initiators are on top of the deck at the aft end of the canopy.

A video camera is also mounted on the left canopy rail, just forward of the rocket motor. The small index pin at the forward corner of the rail is visible as a small point at the right edge of the photograph.

F/A-18F

An F/A-18F from Fleet Replenishment Squadron VFA-122 flies over the mountains of California. This Super Hornet is BuNo. 165670, which was the ninth F/A-18F built. Note that it has the "pizza box" on the nose and the cable guard under the aft fuselage. (Boeing)

The original Hornet variant was the F/A-18A, and 371 were produced, not counting the Full Scale Production (FSD) aircraft. Concurrently, forty two-seat F/A-18Bs were delivered, and although these retained full combat capabilities, they have been used exclusively in training roles. These F/A-18Bs were essentially F/A-18As with a second cockpit in tandem to the first. To make room for the second cockpit, internal fuel capacity was reduced, and several pieces of equipment were relocated. The second single-seat version was the F/A-18C, and the corresponding two-seat version was the F/A-18D. Again, the Navy used the F/A-18D as a trainer, but the Marines developed a specialized ground attack version. This became the first two-seat variant of the Hornet to be assigned to operational squadrons and fly combat missions. Marine squadron VMFA(AW)-121 flew F/A-18Ds in Operation Desert Storm, and other F/A-18Ds took part in Operation Iraqi Freedom. Nevertheless, far more F/A-18Cs were produced than F/A-18Ds.

This philosophy has changed with the two Super Hornet variants. The two-seat F/A-18F is considered to be on an equal footing with the F/A-18E. The F/A-18F is intended to replace the F-14 Tomcat as the Navy's fleet defense interceptor, and it will also take on the attack capability assumed by the F-14 in the early 1990s. The present schedule calls for all F-14 Tomcats to be replaced by Super Hornets by the end of 2007.

Interestingly, the Naval Flight Officer (NFO) in the rear cockpit of the F/A-18F is called the Weapon Systems Officer (WSO) rather than the Radar Intercept Officer (RIO) as he was in the F-14 Tomcat. This is in line with the F/A-18D where the crewman in the rear cockpit is also known as the WSO.

To make room for the second cockpit, the internal fuel capacity had to be reduced by 138 gallons. Accordingly, the F/A-18F is often seen with more external fuel tanks than the F/A-18F. Otherwise, the performance figures for the two Super Hornet variants are almost identical. Further, the F/A-18F has the full combat capabilities as the F/A-18E, and it can employ all of the same weapons. All upgrades made to the F/A-18E will be made to the F/A-18F, and additionally, the F/A-18F is scheduled to receive an enhanced crew station in the rear cockpit.

The F/A-18F will be the first two-seat version of the Hornet to be built in approximately equal numbers to its sin-

Armed with an AGM-88 HARM, an F/A-18F from VX-9 is ready for a mission with an Air Force F-16C Fighting Falcon assigned to Hill Air Force Base, Utah. (Boeing)

An F/A-18F from VX-23 is ready to be launched from the Navy's newest aircraft carrier, USS RONALD REAGAN, CVN-76, on July 25, 2003. (U. S. Navy)

gle-seat counterpart and considered to have equal capabilities as a combat aircraft. Its airframe will also be used to develop the EA-18G Growler electronic warfare aircraft.

The first fleet squadron to become operational with the F/A-18F was VFA-41, a former Tomcat squadron which reached its IOC in 2002. In early 2003, VFA-41 deployed with its sister F/A-18E squadron aboard USS NIMITZ, CVN-68, and headed for the Persian Gulf. On the F/A-18F's first deployment the squadron participated in Operation Iraqi Freedom. It also flew the first missions with the SHARP reconnaissance pod system.

VFA-102 and VFA-2 have also turned in their Tomcats for F/A-18Fs, and VFA-102 has become the first Super Hornet squadron to be permanently deployed outside the United States. As part of Carrier Air Wing Five assigned to USS KITTY HAWK, CV-63, VFA-102 is based at NAF Atsugi, Japan. KITTY HAWK is based at nearby Yokosuka.

An F/A-18F assigned to VFA-102 taxis to the ramp after landing at Naval Air Facility Atsugi, Japan, on November 13, 2003. The photograph was taken in the fading light of the evening, and the formation light panels are turned on. VFA-102 is assigned to Carrier Air Wing Five (CVW-5) aboard USS KITTY HAWK, CV-63, and it is the first Super Hornet squadron to be permanently home based outside the United States. (U. S. Navy)

F/A-18F CANOPY DETAILS

Above: The only external difference between the F/A-18E and the F/A-18F is the longer canopy covering the second cockpit. This top view shows the slightly bulbous shape of the canopy. (Boeing)

Left: The windscreen is the same as the one used on the F/A-18E.

Below: The long canopy has only one lateral brace between the cockpits, and this provides great visibility for both crewmen. (Boeing)

The windscreen on both the F/A-18E and F/A-18F is hinged at the forward end to provide access to wiring and equipment beneath the coaming.

The inside of the framework on the windscreen is painted flat black. Note that it also has an airtight seal to insure cockpit pressurization.

The F/A-18F's canopy has rear-view mirrors at the leading edge and also on the lateral frame for the rear cockpit. Again, note the pressurization seal under the rails.

As on the F/A-18E, video cameras and Canopy Jettison Rocket Motors are located on both sides of the canopy frame.

The Canopy Actuation Connecting Link is shorter on the F/A-18F than on the F/A-18E. The Rocket Motor Initiators and the Canopy Latch Thruster are directly under the glass on top of the deck between the canopy rails.

The Canopy Actuator is mounted on a support structure and located directly behind the rear ejection seat. It moves the connecting link which in turn raises and lowers the canopy.

E/F-18G GROWLER

The ubiquitous F1 was also used as a demonstrator for the proposed EA-18G. It is shown here with five ECM pods, two AGM-88 HARM anti-radiation missiles, two AIM-120 AMRAAM air-to-air missiles, and one AIM-9M Sidewinder missile. Real EA-18Gs will have the ALQ-218 pods on both wing tips instead of just the right wing tip as shown in this photograph. (Boeing)

The EA-6B Prowler electronic warfare aircraft has been in service since the final years of the Vietnam War. Constant upgrades have kept it current with the present threats, but the airframe is reaching the end of its service life. Plans are to replace these aircraft with a specialized version of the Super Hornet which has been designated the EA-18G. Combining the G suffix with the Prowler's name has resulted in the name "Growler" being bestowed on this future version of the Super Hornet. Like the Prowler, the EA-18G will carry external electronic countermeasures (ECM) pods and will employ the HARM anti-radiation missile. Pods on the wingtips will contain antennas for the ALQ-218 system which will replace the ALQ-99 used in the Prowler.

Advances in electronics will mean that the two-seat EA-18G will operate just as effectively as the present four-seat EA-6B. Further, the Growler will be able to defend itself with AIM-120 AMRAAM missiles, and it will have a much higher speed than the EA-6B. These features will increase the survivability of the aircraft.

Another advantage of using the Super Hornet's airframe to create the Navy's new electronic warfare aircraft is that it will have many parts in common with the F/A-18E and F/A-18F. This reduces unit costs and simplifies logistics, maintenance, training, and other support issues.

F/A-18F number 1 was fitted with various configurations of ECM pods and AGM-88 HARM missiles, and it was test flown with these stores in place. It has been photographed as a demonstrator and publicity aircraft for the Growler concept. As of this writing, no production EA-18Gs have been completed, but in 2009, they will begin to replace the EA-6B Prowler on the flight decks of the Navy's aircraft carriers.

F1 is shown here with fuel tanks in place of two of the ECM pods shown above. This combination of tanks, pods, and HARMs is probably more typical of what the EA-18G will carry once it enters service. (Boeing)

OPERATION ENDURING FREEDOM

VFA-115's first cruise with the F/A-18E was in support of Operation Enduring Freedom. Operating from USS ABRAHAM LINCOLN, CVN-72, the squadron flew the Super Hornet's first combat missions. The CAG aircraft with its black tail and yellow markings is visible in the foreground. It has a GBU-31 Joint Direct Attack Munition (JDAM) on Station 8. (U. S. Navy)

Not since the Korean War has a Navy squadron made its initial carrier deployment in a new jet fighter knowing it would see combat during the cruise. But that is exactly what happened when the Eagles of VFA-115 embarked aboard USS ABRAHAM LINCOLN, CVN-72, in late July 2002. As part of Carrier Air Wing Fourteen, VFA-115 became the first operational squadron equipped with Super Hornets to make a deployment aboard a carrier. As they left the west coast of the United States behind, they knew that they would fly combat missions in Afghanistan as part of Operation Enduring Freedom. What they did not know was that the cruise would be extended, and they would also participate in Operation Iraqi Freedom before they returned home from the longest carrier deployment in many years.

From September 13 until October 20, 2002, VFA-115 successfully accomplished ninety out of ninety assigned missions in support of Operation Enduring Freedom, ranging deep into Afghanistan to deliver Joint Direct Attack Munitions, laser guided bombs, and standard bombs against the Taliban and al Quaida. LINCOLN then moved to a position off Iraq, and the Eagles flew all five of their assigned missions enforcing UN resolutions as part of Operation Southern Watch on October 29.

During missions over Afghanistan, F/A-18Es often carried a weapons load consisting of one GBU-16 laser guided bomb on Station 3, and four 500-pound bombs on CVERS mounted on Stations 7 and 8. A "Nite Hawk" FLIR pod was loaded on Station 5. For defense against hostile aircraft, two AIM-9Ms were carried on the wing tip stations, and one AIM-120 AMRAAM missile was loaded on Station 7. A 480-gallon fuel tank was on the centerline station. The drum for the cannon was loaded with 350 rounds of 20-mm ammunition. One of VFA-115's F/A-18Es with this weapons loading is shown in the photograph on page 3.

Depending on many factors, including the range to the target and the type of target being attacked, other weapons loads were also carried. Two GBU-31 2,000-pound Joint Direct Attack Munitions (JDAM) were often loaded on Stations 4 and 8, and an FPU-11 external fuel tank was carried on the centerline station. For strike missions, a "Nite Hawk" FLIR pod on Station 5, an AIM-120 AMRAAM on Station 7, and two AIM-9M Sidewinders on the wing tip stations remained standard regardless of what weapons were carried to destroy the assigned targets on the ground.

Throughout Operation Enduring Freedom, the F/A-18Es typically carried a heavier weapons load than either the F/A-18C or the F-14D. The only area where the Super Hornet fell short in this respect was that it was loaded with only 350 rounds of 20mm ammunition as compared to 500 rounds in both the F/A-18C and F-14D. This was accomplished in spite of the fact that weapons separation testing was still underway for the Super Hornet, and the aircraft was restricted to using only those loads that had already been certified. During Operation Enduring Freedom, the GBU-35 1,000-pound JDAM and the GBU-12 500-pound laser guided bomb were not certified for use on the Super Hornet. Further, only two GBU-16 1,000-pound bombs were certified to be carried, and this will be increased to four. Once these and other

27

With a GBU-31 JDAM beneath its wing, an F/A-18E launches from one of LINCOLN's waist catapults for a mission over Afghanistan on October 12, 2002. (U. S. Navy)

weapons are certified for use in different combinations, the lethality and flexibility of the Super Hornet will be significantly increased.

VFA-115's F/A-18Es also served as armed mission tankers in OEF. This is a role that legacy Hornets cannot perform, and it significantly increased the air wing's combat capability and flexibility. In this role, the F/A-18Es carried a D704 aerial refueling store on the centerline station and two FPU-11 480-gallon fuel tanks on Stations 4 and 8. One AIM-120 was carried on Station 7, and two AIM-9Ms were loaded on the wing tip launch rails. When used as an "overhead"

One of VFA-115's F//A-18Es returns to LINCOLN after flying a sortie as an armed mission tanker. A D704 refueling store is on the centerline station, while FPU-11 480-gallon external fuel tanks are on Stations 5 and 8. Two AIM-9M Sidewinders are carried on the wing tips, and one AIM-120 AMRAAM is loaded on Station 7 for defense against enemy aircraft. (U. S. Navy)

The squadron commander's aircraft taxis forward on the flight deck with a GBU-16 laser guided bomb on Station 3. AIM-9M Sidewinders are on Stations 1 and 11. An eagle insignia is painted on the nose and is symbolic of Operation Enduring Freedom. (U. S. Navy)

tanker in close proximity to the carrier, the number of external fuel tanks was usually increased from two to four.

VFA-115 deployed aboard LINCOLN with twelve F/A-18Es. Throughout Operations Enduring Freedom and Southern Watch, they maintained a mission capable rate of eighty-seven percent. This means that at least ten of their Super Hornets were usually ready to fly a mission.

As the men and women aboard LINCOLN neared the scheduled completion of their deployment, they looked forward to returning home. But world events would delay their homecoming when the ship was ordered to turn around and return to the Persian Gulf to support the impending invasion of Iraq. There would be more combat missions for Carrier Air Wing Fourteen to fly as part of Operation Iraqi Freedom before the carrier returned to the United States.

An F/A-18E from VFA-115 is chained to LINCOLN's flight deck between missions. Notice that the two AIM-9M Sidewinders and single AIM-120 AMRAAM remain in place. (U. S. Navy)

OPERATION IRAQI FREEDOM

Armed with two JDAMs and two Sidewinders, an F/A-18E from VFA-115 prepares to launch for a mission over Iraq on March 25, 2003.

When Operation Iraqi Freedom began, five aircraft carriers were on station in the Persian Gulf and Mediterranean Sea. Of these, only LINCOLN had a squadron of Super Hornets. A sixth carrier, USS NIMITZ, was on its way to the Persian Gulf, and it had one F/A-18E and one F/A-18F squadron in Carrier Air Wing Eleven.

VFA-115 flew missions in support of the war beginning on the very first night, and as NIMITZ steamed across the Indian Ocean to the war zone, two F/A-18Es from VFA-14 and two F/A-18Fs from VFA-41 were prepared to fly from NIMITZ to LINCOLN to increase Carrier Air Wing Fourteen's fighter and tanker capabilities. CDR A. E. Ross, commanding officer of VFA-14, selected LCDR Hal Schmitt and LCDR Jason Norris to fly the two F/A-18Es to LINCOLN. The CO

of VFA-41, CDR Pat Cleary, chose LCDR Mark Weisgerberger and LCDR Brian Garrison to fly the F/A-18Fs. Their crewmen would be LT Tom Poulter and LT Tom Bodine.

Each of the four Super Hornets were loaded with five external fuel tanks as they launched from NIMITZ and headed for LINCOLN in the Persian Gulf. The first leg of their journey was 1,700 miles and they were refuelled during the flight from tankers operating from NIMITZ. The second leg was 2,300 miles, and it involved another in-flight refueling before the four aircraft finally landed aboard LINCOLN.

Once aboard LINCOLN, the two Super Hornets from VFA-41 made history by flying the F/A-18F's first combat missions. All four aircraft were serviced by personnel assigned to VFA-115 while they operated from LINCOLN.

On March 25, 2003, NIMITZ arrived in the Persian Gulf and began air operations against Iraq. The four Super Hornets returned to their assigned carrier where they continued operations with their squadrons.

During Operation Iraqi Freedom, flight operations continued around the clock. One of VFA-115's F/A-18Es is prepared for a night launch on March 23, 2003. The Super Hornet is configured for an aerial refueling mission with four external fuel tanks under its wings. A D704 refueling store is on the centerline station. Note the glow of the formation light panels on the nose, aft fuselage, and vertical tails. The upper beacon flashes brightly on the vertical tail as the pilot applies power to the engines. (U. S. Navy)

One of the F/A-18Es from VFA-14 aboard USS NIMITZ, CVN-68, is respotted on the flight deck of USS ABRAHAM LINCOLN after flying almost 4,000 miles to reach LINCOLN which was already participating in Operation Iraqi Freedom. (U. S. Navy)

GBU-16 laser guided bombs and GBU-31 JDAMs were among the weapons employed by Super Hornets during Operation Iraqi Freedom. Photographs also show that GBU-12 500-pound laser guided bombs were also added to the Super Hornet's arsenal by the time OIF began. Mk 82 500-pound bombs and Mk 83 1,000-pound bombs were also delivered in relatively high numbers, but the Mk 84 2000-pound bomb was seldom used as a free-fall weapon.

Instead the warhead was usually fitted with a JDAM guidance kit to become a GBU-31. During Operation Iraqi Freedom, Super Hornets also continued to serve as tankers for the other aircraft in the air wings aboard LINCOLN and NIMITZ.

After President Bush announced an end to the major combat phase of Operation Iraqi Freedom aboard LINCOLN as she finally returned home, NIMITZ and her air wing remained on deployment until November 2003. During the months she remained at sea, the first Shared Reconnaissance Pod (SHARP) arrived aboard NIMITZ. VFA-41 began flying missions with this new system that will eventually make the Super Hornet the Navy's primary carrier-borne reconnaissance asset.

Two F/A-18Fs from VFA-41 also flew from NIMITZ to LINCOLN so that they could participate in Operation Iraqi Freedom while NIMITZ continued to steam toward the Persian Gulf. After reaching LINCOLN, the two aircraft from the Black Aces became the first F/A-18Fs to fly combat missions. While aboard LINCOLN, the Super Hornets from both VFA-14 and VFA-41 were serviced by personnel assigned to VFA-115. One of VFA-41's F/A-18Fs is shown here just after having flown its first combat mission on April 1, 2003. Ordnancemen stand ready to upload GBU-16 laser guided bombs onto the aircraft in preparation for its next mission. (U. S. Navy)

Above: Armed with four GBU-12 500-pound laser guided bombs, an F/A-18F from VFA-41 is hooked up to Cat Two aboard USS NIMITZ, CVN-68, for a mission over Iraq on March 28, 2003. Although two of VFA-41's Super Hornets had flown the F/A-18F's first combat missions a few days earlier from USS ABRAHAM LINCOLN, the first combat operations by a full F/A-18F squadron were flown by VFA-41 from NIMITZ. The carrier had arrived in the Persian Gulf and begun operations in support of Operation Iraqi Freedom only three days before this photo was taken. (U. S. Navy)

Below: An F/A-18E from VFA-115 launches from USS ABRAHAM LINCOLN for a mission over Iraq on March 28. A typical load of external stores for F/A-18Es during both Operation Enduring Freedom and Operation Iraqi Freedom included AIM-9M Sidewinders on the wing tips, a GBU-16 laser guided bomb on Station 3, an FPU-11 fuel tank on Station 6, two Mk 83/BSU-85 1,000-pound bombs on a CVER on Station 8, and one Mk 83/BSU on Station 9. Not visible is a TFLIR pod on the left fuselage cheek station. LAU-127 launch rails are on Stations 2 and 10, but these are empty. (U. S. Navy)

SUPER HORNET COLORS

F/A-18E, BuNo. 165168, was used for a wide variety of flight testing.

The sixth F/A-18E, BuNo. 165533, was also the first LRIP I Super Hornet delivered.

The same F/A-18E illustrated above later became the squadron commander's aircraft for VX-9.

This F/A-18E, BuNo. 165537, was assigned to VX-23 and used for weapons separations tests.

F/A-18F, BuNo. 165884, was assigned to the Black Aces of VFA-41 aboard USS NIMITZ, CVN-68.

F/A-18E COLORS

The Replacement Air Group (RAG) is VFA-122 based at NAS Lemoore, California, about thirty miles south of Fresno. The RAG is also called the Fleet Replenishment Squadron (FRS). There is a RAG squadron for each type of aircraft operational with the fleet, and the mission of the squadron is to train pilots that will be assigned to fly the aircraft in fleet and test squadrons. VFA-122 trains pilots in both the F/A-18E and F/A-18F Super Hornet. The aircraft in the foreground is the squadron commander's aircraft and it, along with the CAG aircraft, has colorful tail markings. All other Super Hornets assigned to the squadron have gray markings on the tails. (Boeing)

Center: The first fleet squadron to become operational with the F/A-18E was VFA-115. Deployed aboard USS ABRAHAM LINCOLN, CVN-72, the squadron also introduced the Super Hornet to combat, flying missions over Afghanistan in support of Operation Enduring Freedom. Later in the same deployment, VFA-115 took part in Operation Southern Watch and Operation Iraqi Freedom. The squadron's CAG aircraft features black vertical tails with yellow and white markings. (U. S. Navy)

Left: The squadron commander's aircraft for VFA-115 has yellow and white markings on its vertical tails, but the tails are not painted black. Tail markings on other VFA-115 aircraft are gray. (U. S. Navy)

The next F/A-18E fleet squadron to become operational was VFA-14. The Tophatters' CAG aircraft had gloss black vertical tails and colorful markings, and it is shown here on the ramp at NAS Lemoore in August 2002 prior to the squadron's first deployment aboard USS NIMITZ, CVN-68. During that initial deployment, VFA-14, a former F-14 Tomcat squadron, flew missions in support of Operation Iraqi Freedom. This is the same F/A-18E pictured on the front cover of this book, however, the cover photograph was taken at an earlier time before the unit's Tophatters emblem was added to the vertical tails.

Center: CDR Bruce "Puppy" Fecht, Commanding Officer of VFA-14 when the unit transitioned to the F/A-18E, flies lead in front of three of the squadron's Super Hornets. The squadron commander's aircraft has red markings and colorful insignias, while the other aircraft carry standard gray markings. (VFA-14)

Right: The left side of the squadron commander's F/A-18E is shown in this photograph that was taken on the ramp at NAS Lemoore in August 2002. Note the tri-color national insignia on the nose of the aircraft just forward of the boarding ladder.

F/A-18F COLORS

Above: An F/A-18F from the RAG squadron, VFA-122, pays a visit to NAS Whidbey Island, Washington, in August 2003.

Left: VFA-41 was the first fleet squadron to become operational in the F/A-18F. As the sister squadron to VFA-14, it deployed aboard USS NIMITZ, CVN-68, and took part in Operation Iraqi Freedom. One of the squadron's Super Hornets is shown here with three external fuel tanks and two cluster bombs as it is readied for launch on a mission over Iraq on April 7, 2003. (U. S. Navy)

Below: Colorful markings are painted on VFA-41's squadron commander's aircraft. The unit's CAG aircraft carries the same markings.

Above: VFA-102 was the second fleet squadron to become operational in the F/A-18F. The squadron is known as the Diamonbacks, and the unit's emblem has a diamondback rattlesnake coiled around a crest. (U. S. Navy)

Right: One of VFA-102's F/A-18Fs gets the signal to launch during carrier qualifications aboard USS JOHN C. STENNIS, CVN-74. (U. S. Navy)

Below: After flying Tomcats during Operation Iraqi Freedom, VFA-2 returned home to begin transitioning to the F/A-18F. The squadron commander's new Super Hornet flies in formation with the CAG F-14 to symbolize the transition. (U. S. Navy)

F/A-18E COCKPIT DETAILS & COLORS

The cockpit in the F/A-18E looks very much like the one in the previous F/A-18C. Information is displayed on large panels, and only a very few standard instruments remain on the panel. Even fuel status is displayed on a screen in the lower left corner of the panel. The Multi-Purpose Display is at the center of the panel directly in front of the control column.

The lower right side of the panel has some standard instruments, all of which have secondary or standby functions. These include a magnetic compass, attitude indicator, altimeter, and vertical velocity indicator. The cockpit's pressure altitude is indicated by the small gage near the floor at the lower right corner of the center panel.

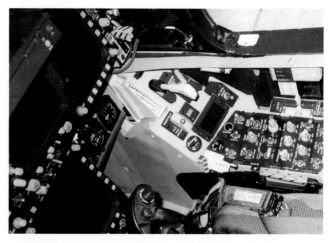

The throttle is the major feature on the left side of the cockpit. Switches just outboard of the throttle are on the Ground Test Panel. Aft of the throttle is the Fuel Control Panel and the Flight Control System Panel.

The handle on the Right Auxiliary Panel operates the arresting hook. The forward panels on the right console are the Electrical Power Panel, the Environmental Control Panel, and the Interior Lights Panel.

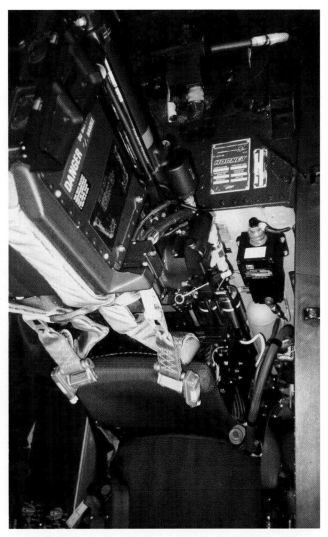

The panel at the aft end of the cockpit on the right side is the Fan Test Control Unit. A switch is used to check the right and left fans. When the switch is in the center position, the unit is off. Night Vision Goggles (NVG) are stored in a container at the aft end of the right console.

Details at the aft end of the cockpit on the left side are revealed here. The black box next to the ejection seat is the Oxygen Monitor. Connections and controls for the pilot's oxygen flow and the anti-G suit are near the aft end of the left console.

The area behind the ejection seat is painted flat black, as is the top of the fuselage where the canopy closes on it. The canopy hinges are shown in this view, as is one of the latches that locks into the fuselage to hold the canopy in place when it is closed.

Several "black boxes" are located beneath the panel behind the ejection seat. Note also the builder's data plate near the front of the panel next to the ejection seat. It has the name "Hornet" on it, and the aircraft's Bureau Number and other data are engraved into it.

F/A-18F COCKPIT DETAILS & COLORS
FRONT COCKPIT

Above: The front cockpit in the F/A-18F is essentially the same as the cockpit in the F/A-18E. The landing gear handle is on the left auxiliary panel, and below it are the controls for the operation of the launch bar and the emergency and parking brake. The red button on the control grip is the A/G Weapon Release Button (Pickle Switch), the Sensor Control is in the center at the top of the control grip, and the Pitch and Roll Trim Control is to the right.

Left: Additional details on the left side of the cockpit are shown here. The red button above the throttle is the ECM Dispenser Button. The panel with the red guarded switch is the Flight Control System Panel, and the radios are controlled from the two panels just aft of it.

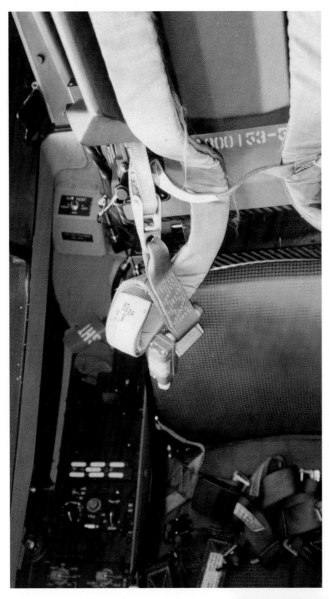

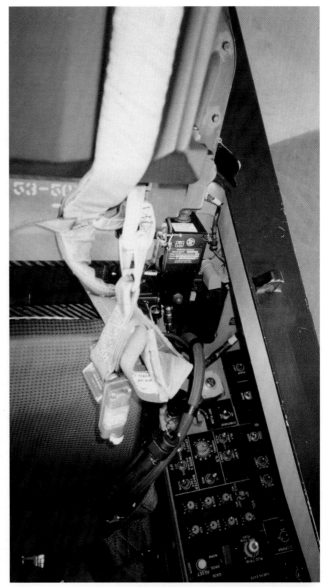

Above left: The aft control panel on the right console is the KY-58 Control Panel. Aft of it is a storage compartment for the Night Vision Goggles, while outboard of the panel is storage for navigational charts.

Above Right: The connection for the anti-G suit is at the aft end of the right console. Forward of it are the Communications Panel and Volume Control Panel.

Right: From front to back on the right console are the Electrical Power Panel, Environment Control System Panel, Air Refueling Store Panel, Sensor Panel, a blank panel, and the KY-58 Control Panel. The utility light, with its coiled power cord, can be seen mounted above the blank panel.

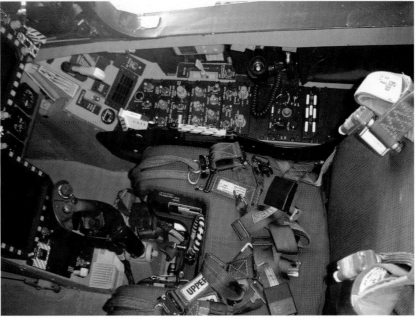

REAR COCKPIT

The instrument panel in the rear cockpit of F/A-18Fs in Lots 21 through 25 is shown here. At the top center of the panel is the Multi-Purpose Color Display (MPCD). Note that the same basic standby instruments as found in the front cockpit are in the lower right corner of the panel. The socket in the center of the floor accepts a control column so that the aircraft can be flown from the rear cockpit, and the small lever just above it is the Rudder Pedal Adjustment. However, being flown as a trainer is a secondary mission of the F/A-18F.

The two photos above show the area aft of the front seat in an F/A-18F that covers the instrument panel. There is a handle mounted on top of the coaming, and of note are the two switches beneath the handle at each end. These two switches activate the chaff/flare dispensers. These dispensers are located under the engine inlets and dispense chaff to jam radars in a threat environment that includes radar-guided surface-to-air missiles. The flares are used to confuse infrared-homing missiles that guide on heat sources.

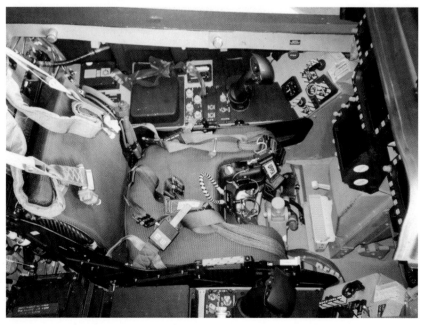

The side consoles in the rear cockpit are completely different from those in the front. A hand controller is located near the forward end of each console. One controller is simply a mirror image of the other, and each can control antenna elevation and the use of flares and chaff. Just aft of the controller is the RECCE Panel and the PTT Panel. Volume controls for the radio are on the small panel just forward of the large blank panel. Next to it is the yellow Canopy Jettison Handle. Aft of the large blank panel are the connections and controls for the pilot's oxygen and anti-G suit. The auxiliary panel forward of the console contains the Emergency Jettison Button, Emergency Landing Gear Handle and Light, Emergency Brake Handle and Light, and the Cockpit Altimeter.

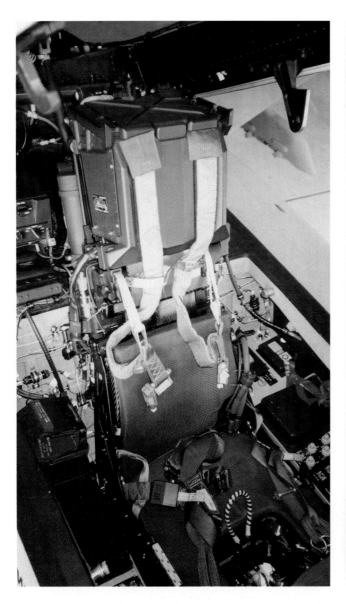

Above left and right: The F/A-18E and F/A-18F are fitted with the NACES SJU-17 ejection seat. The SJU-17(V)1/A is located in the cockpit of the F/A-18E, the SJU-17(V)2/A is the front seat in the F/A-18F, and the SJU-17(V)1A is in the aft cockpit. These seats are externally identical. The SJU-17(V)2A has provisions for dual ejection required for the F/A-18F. This provides a time separation between the forward and aft seats to avoid interference during the ejection sequence.

Right: The auxiliary panel on the right side of the cockpit has Hydraulic Pressure Indicators, a Seat Caution Mode Switch, a Command Selector Valve, and the Caution Light Panel. Aft of the right controller is the Interior Light Panel.

ADVANCED CREW STATION

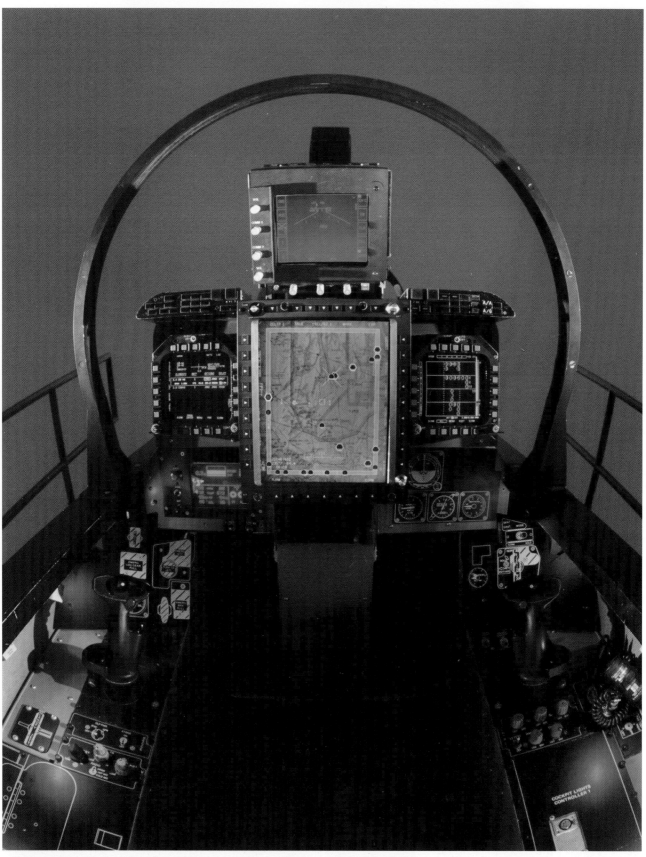

Although the Super Hornet is the Navy's newest combat aircraft, future improvements are already well underway. Among them is an advanced crew station for the rear cockpit in the F/A-18F. Compare this photograph to the ones taken in a present F/A-18F on the previous two pages. Notice the new large displays on the instrument panel and that the two side controllers remain at the forward end of the two consoles. (Boeing)

F414-GE-400 ENGINE DETAILS & COLORS

The F/A-18E and F/A-18F are powered by two General Electric F414-GE-400 engines, each of which produces 22,000 pounds of thrust. These two photos look into the aft end of each engine and show the flame holders and the convergent/divergent nozzle. Note that the "turkey feather" covers are in place over the nozzle's actuators.

Above and below: Details of the F414-GE-400 turbofan engine are revealed in these two views. (Boeing photos)

AN/APG-65 RADAR

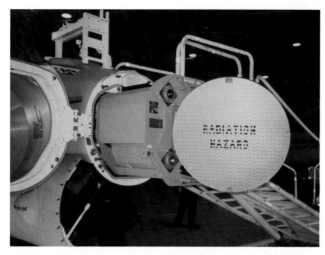

Early production Super Hornets have the same AN/APG-65 radar used in the earlier versions of the Hornet. An improved radar, designated the AN/APG-79, is under development to replace the AN/APG-65 in the not-too-distant future.

The radar antenna and much of its associated equipment slides out on rails for maintenance. The AN/APG-65 radar has an antenna that moves mechanically to direct the beam, but the future AN/APG-79 will have a much faster electronically scanned beam.

In this photograph, the radar has been pushed back into the nose. The hinge for the radome is also visible in this view.

The antenna is simply a flat circular disc, and it has no dipoles extending from its forward face. The cannon muzzle faring is directly above the radar.

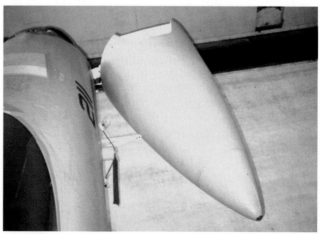

The interior of the radome is a beige color, while the frame where it mates to the fuselage is gloss white. Note the flat area at the top of the radome.

A V-shaped brace between the radome and the fuselage holds the radome in the open position. The cannon muzzle faring fits into the indented flat area at the top.

AVIONICS BAYS

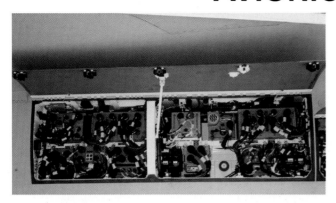

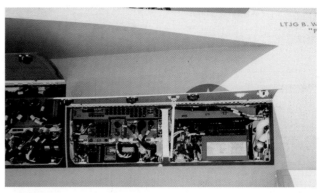

Much of the electrical equipment is located in easily accessible bays on both sides of the forward fuselage. On the right side, Bay 4R (to the left in the photo) contains the Mission Computer and Flight Control Computer on the top shelf, and the Signal Data Computer and Stores Management Processor on the lower shelf. To the right, Bay 3R has the TACAN, HARM Command Launch Computer, and the Flight Control Computer on the top shelf. The Havequick Sincgars Radio, Communication Systems Control, Pulse Decoder Rate Gyro, and Interference Blanker are on the lower shelf.

Bay 2R, which is the aft bay of the two smaller equipment bays, contains Power Distribution Panels Numbers 6 and 8, the Anti-Skid Unit, Environmental Control System Controller, and a Transformer Rectifier. A small Power Transformer is in the lower aft corner of the bay. Bay 1R, which is the forward-most bay, contains Power Distribution Panels Numbers 2 and 4, a Current Transformer, and a magenta colored battery. It should be noted that the four photos on this page were taken in the bays of two F/A-18Es, but the locations for the equipment in the F/A-18F are the same.

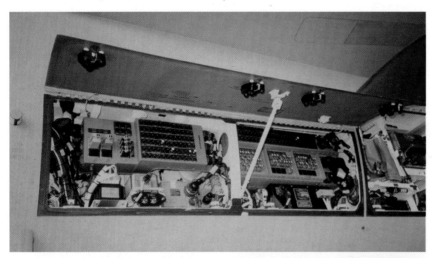

Bay 1L is the forward-most bay on the left side of the forward fuselage. The major item in this bay is Power Distribution Panel Number 1, and below it is the External Power Monitor LCS Service Panel. Bay 2L contains Power Distribution Panel Number 5, and below it is the Transformer Rectifier. In this, and the other photographs on this page, note that the interior of the bays is painted gloss white, as are the braces that hold the access doors in the open position. The inside surface of the doors is an olive green color, while most of the equipment is black or dark gray.

Bays 3L, 4L, and 5L are the larger bays further aft on the left side of the aircraft. The green item in Bay 3L is the Onboard Oxygen Generating System (OBOGS) Concentrator. Below it is Power Distribution Panel Number 9. The yellow box on the top shelf is the Ring Laser Gyro Inertial Navigation Unit, and just aft of it is the Mission Computer. Below the Navigation Unit is the APX-100, and next to it is the ALR-67 Computer. The other two items on the lower shelf in Bay 3L are the KIT-1A and Power Distribution Panel 7. Bay 4L contains the Airborne Self-Protection Jammer and Power Distribution Panel Number 11, while Bay 5L is empty to allow equipment to be added in the future.

M61 VULCAN 20-MM CANNON

Since the 1950s, many American fighters have been armed with the M61 Vulcan cannon. This is the cannon as installed in the F/A-18E and F/A-18F. Note the ammunition feed chutes on the right side of the weapon.

As installed in the Super Hornet, the gun system can be loaded with a maximum of 412 rounds. This compares to 570 rounds in earlier Hornets. The reduction is to provide space for future equipment additions.

The cannon fires through a natural metal muzzle fairing on the top of the nose where the radome mates with the fuselage. The small intakes on each side of the muzzle take in air to purge gun gasses from inside the forward fuselage compartment.

The cannon system is installed in the forward fuselage compartment with the ammunition drum being just aft of the retracted radar. To remove the cannon, the radar is pulled forward on its rails, and the cannon is winched down out of the compartment.

SUPER HORNET DETAILS

JHMCS HELMET

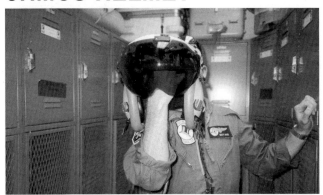

The Joint Helmet-Mounted Cueing System (JHMCS) is intended to be used with the AIM-9X Sidewinder missile. The pilot looks at the target he wishes to engage, and electronics in the helmet sends information to the missile. The missile then locks onto that target and engages it after launch. This system is much faster and offers a much wider field of engagement than with previous versions of the Sidewinder which required the pilot to point his aircraft at the target and get a tone from the missile's seeker head before engaging. The six photographs on this page show the new JHMCS helmet from all aspects.

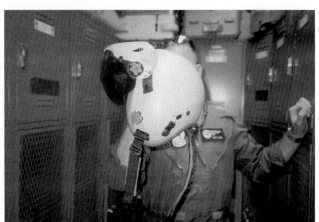

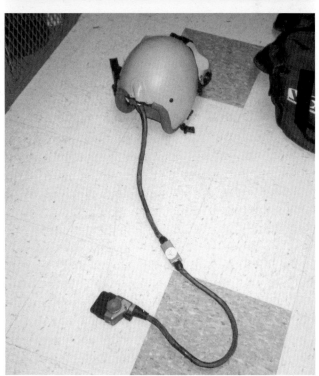

PILOT'S FLIGHT GEAR

Except for the JHMCS helmet, Super Hornet pilots and Naval Flight Officers wear flight gear that is essentially the same as that worn by their counterparts who fly ear- *lier versions of the Hornet. In these four photos, LTJG Matt Dick of VFA-14, poses in his flight suit, anti-G suit, and emergency survival equipment.*

RETRACTABLE BOARDING LADDER

The aft brace is visible in this view of the ladder extended from an F/A-18F. The ladder folds down flat as it is closed into the well in the underside of the left leading edge extension. The ladder is painted gloss white and has flat black non-skid surfaces on each rung.

Like the earlier versions of the Hornet, the F/A-18E and F/A-18F have a self-contained boarding ladder that extends down from a well inside the left leading edge extension. Note the V-shaped brace between the ladder and the fuselage.

When closed, the ladder is covered by two doors. The long door is on the forward side of the ladder itself, and a short door is at the front end of the well.

The interior of the well and where the ladder and aft brace mount into it are revealed here. Note the latch which holds the ladder in place when it is retracted.

LANDING GEAR DETAIL

The landing gear used on the Super Hornet is the same basic design used on earlier versions of the Hornet, but there are some detail differences. In this right side view, notice the torque link extending aft from the strut between the two nose gear wheels. The struts and wheels are painted gloss white. The nose gear retracts forward into its well.

The catapult launch bar extends forward from the strut, and it is hooked into the catapult shuttle when the Super Hornet is launched from an aircraft carrier. The nose gear structure must be strong enough to withstand the stress of the catapult accelerating the entire weight of the aircraft from zero to flying speed in just over two seconds.

A front view of the nose landing gear shows the stance of the gear on its dual wheels with the oleo portion of the strut between them. The landing/taxi light is high on the strut, and the three approach indicator lights are mounted vertically in a small box below it.

A rear view shows the aft door attached to the drag link. Also note the angle of the three other doors in this photograph. The nose gear is steerable, allowing the Super Hornet to be maneuvered in the limited spaces available on the flight deck of an aircraft carrier.

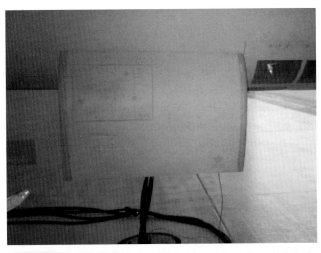

The nose gear well is covered by four doors when it is in the retracted position. This is the forward right door as seen from the outside. The rectangle painted in the upper left quarter of the door contains basic servicing information for the ground crew.

The forward left door is the same length as the forward right door, but it is not as big in the vertical dimension. The forward two doors cover the wide portion of the gear well that houses the dual wheels when the landing gear is retracted.

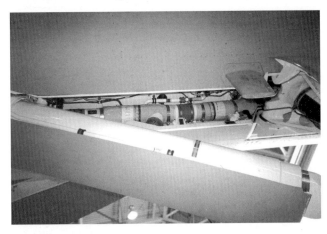

The drag link fits into the aft end of the well when the gear is retracted. This part of the well is long and narrow, and it is covered by the door that is attached to the bottom of the drag link. The interior of the gear wells is painted gloss white.

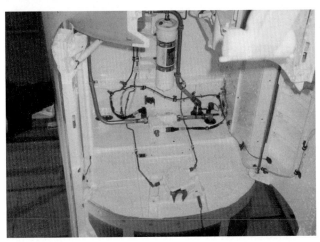

This view looks up and forward into the front of the nose gear well. The dual wheels fit up into this wider area of the well when they retract.

Details inside the forward and center areas of the nose gear well are revealed in this photo that looks aft. Note the arms that open and close the doors.

LEFT LANDING GEAR

Like the nose landing gear, the Super Hornet's main landing gear is the same basic design used on legacy Hornets. This is the left landing gear as viewed from the front quarter.

A major design change from the earlier Hornet variants can be seen in this photograph. The main gear doors have angled or sawtooth edges to increase the stealth characteristics of the Super Hornet.

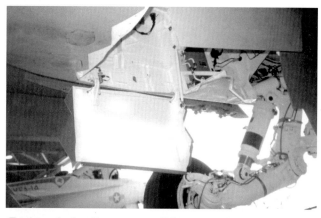

Each main landing gear well is covered by three doors when the gear is retracted. This is the inside surface of the outer aft door. The sharp edges of all gear doors are painted red on the inside surfaces.

This is the outside surface of the same door seen in the photograph at left. The zig-zag leading and trailing edges are clearly visible. Part of the inside surface of the forward gear door is also visible.

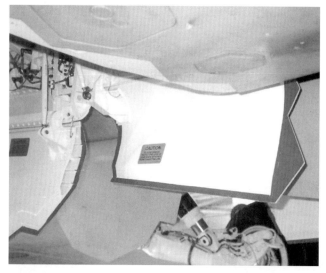

This is the inside surface of the inner aft gear door. The door's forward hinge and actuating rod are visible. Note the white recessed area in the underside of the fuselage that accepts the sawtooth edge of the door.

The oleo portion of the strut and the inside of the left gear wheel are visible in this photograph. Several hydraulic lines run down the lower strut to the brake assembly.

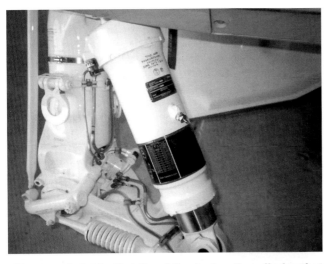

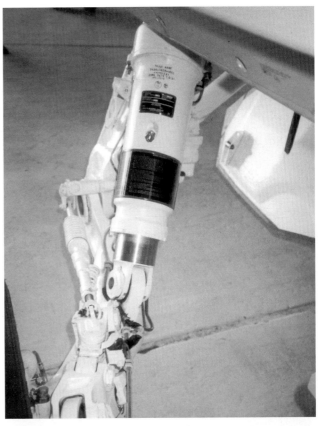

Above and right: Details of the hydraulic cylinder that acts as the shock absorber for the landing gear are revealed in these two views. Black placards provide servicing information for the cylinder.

Below left: The gear strut is mounted at the forward end of the well and the gear retracts aft.

Below right: As the main landing gear retracts, the wheel twists approximately ninety degrees so that it fits flat into the aft end of the well.

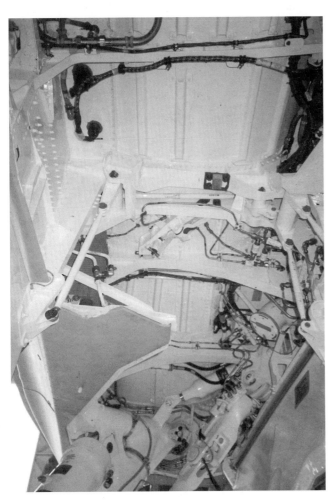

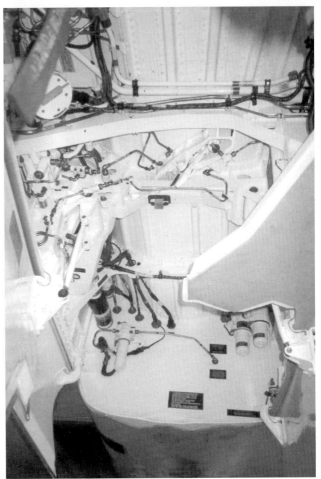

RIGHT LANDING GEAR

The leading edge and inside surface of the forward door is visible in this front view of the right main landing gear. This large door covers the forward part of the well where the strut is mounted to the airframe. Note that the door has the stealthy angled edges and that it hangs at a slight angle rather than straight down. The arm that retracts and extends the gear is visible to the inside of the main strut. Like most carrier-based aircraft, the tires on the Super Hornet have a circumferential tread. Note the two rectangular holes in the underside of the fuselage just forward of the gear well. These are for the chaff/flare dispensers which are part of the self-protection countermeasures carried by the aircraft.

This photo provides a good look at the irregular shape of the leading and trailing edges of the outer gear door. Only the inside edge of the door is straight, and there are no right angles which increase radar signature.

The main strut of each landing gear is hinged with a hydraulic strut between the two sections. The hinge is visible here as are the oleo, hydraulic brake lines, and the brake on the inside of the right wheel.

The forward door for each main landing gear has a very irregular shape. As illustrated in the top photo on this page, the leading edge has a sawtooth design, but the rest of the door is also a series of various angles. Also note the inside of the outer aft door in this low view.

A low rear view of the right landing gear provides a good look at additional details. Note how the hydraulic lines run up into the gear well. The landing gear is painted gloss white so that any leaks of fluids will quickly show, and they are easily cleaned off the gloss paint.

The irregular shape of the forward door is in the left foreground of this photo that looks outward toward the aft outer door. The red on the leading and trailing edges is visible.

The two inner doors on the right main landing gear are shown here, as is the forward door for the left gear. The forward doors have a large hinge and an actuating arm at each end.

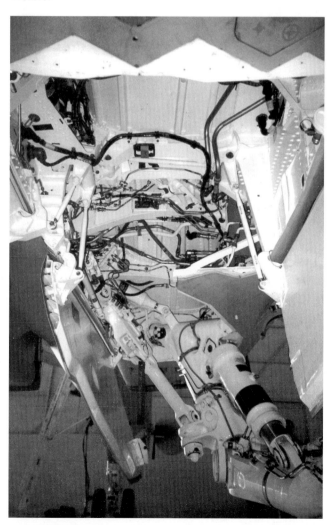

The retraction mechanism for each main landing gear is rather complicated. The main strut rotates aft and slightly inboard to move into the narrow area between the forward and aft sections of the gear well. The retraction arm also rotates the wheel and tire ninety degrees as it retracts and extends.

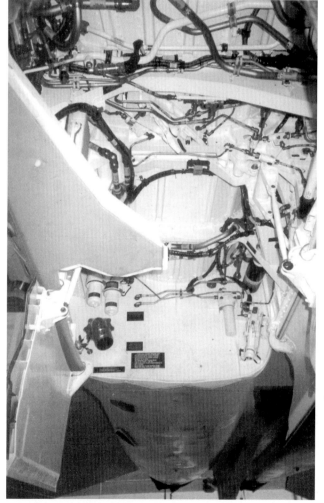

Taken from directly beneath the main gear strut, this view looks back and up into the right gear well. Note the hinges and the actuating links that open and close the two aft gear doors. The outer door is larger in vertical height than the inner door. The interior of the well is a maze of black and natural metal wiring and plumbing.

FUSELAGE DETAILS

Details on the right side of the nose include a formation light panel, an angle-of-attack sensor and a pitot head. Note also the gun gas vents between the nose gear door and the pitot head.

The left side of the nose also has a formation light panel, an angle-of-attack sensor, a pitot probe, and gun gas vents. The open panel just aft of the modex is the Ammunition Load Door.

Like legacy Hornets, Super Hornets have a retractable in-flight refueling probe on the upper right side of the nose. The probe is shown here partially extended with the forward door still in the open position.

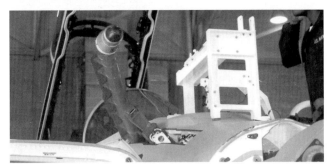

In this view, the refueling probe is in the fully extended position, and the forward door has closed. Except for the nozzle, the probe is painted red, as is the inside surface of the aft door which is attached to the probe.

A close-up provides a better look at the left angle-of-attack sensor and its diamond-shaped panel. The item on top of the nose is known as the "pizza box" and it contains the Combined Interrogator/Transponder (CIT).

The External Electrical Receptacle is located on the left side of the nose just aft of the Ammunition Load Door. The small extended cylinder just forward of it is the Gun Safe Switch.

The Ground Refueling Receptacle is located on the right side of the nose. Located under the same small panel is an intercom connection where a ground crew member can plug in a headset and talk to the pilot.

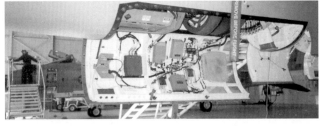

A large door under the forward fuselage provides access to the cannon. The entire cannon system is removed and installed through this door. A considerable amount of equipment is mounted on the inside of the door.

The feature that most easily distinguishes the Super Hornets from the earlier Hornet versions is the change made to the engine inlets. To provide sufficient air to the more powerful F414-GE-400 engines, Super Hornets have large box-like intakes instead of the much smaller rounded inlets found on legacy Hornets.

Under each inlet, and directly in front of the main landing gear are two square openings. Inserts with twenty-four circular holes are placed in the openings, and these contain chaff bundles to deceive enemy radars and flares to confuse infrared-guided missiles. These are part of the aircraft's self-protection system. (Bartolacci)

The hundreds of small holes in the inside wall of the inlet help control the boundary layer air. Air pulled through these holes is used to perform a pre-cooling function for air going into the Environmental Control System by way of a heat exchanger. Vents in the side and top of the inlet are also used to control the airflow.

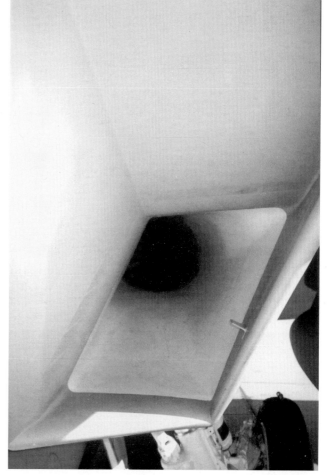

The forward end of the interior of each inlet is painted the same color as the exterior of the aircraft, but most of the ducting leading back to the forward end of the engine is painted flat white. There is a small strake on the outer wall of each inlet which is about six inches long and one and one-half inches high.

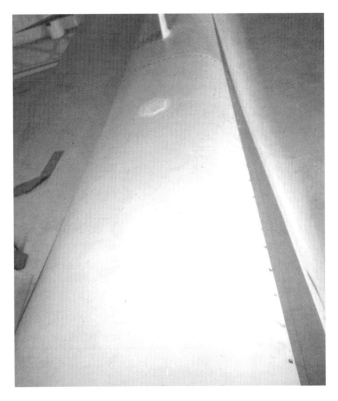

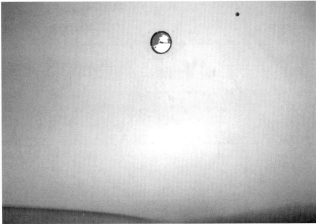

Left: There are two white antennas mounted flush with the top of the fuselage spine. The forward antenna is for the Global Positioning System (GPS), while the one further aft is the Identification Friend Or Foe (IFF) Antenna. The slanted blade antenna at the extreme top of the photo is the VHF/UHF/L Band antenna.

Above: On each side of the aft fuselage is a small gage for the hydraulic reservoirs located inside the aircraft at this point. This is the gage on the left side.

A three-segment formation light panel is located on each side of the rear fuselage between the horizontal tail and the trailing edge of the flap. The aircraft type and Bureau Number is painted beneath the horizontal tail.

A flush-mounted scoop takes in cooling air for the aft fuselage. This is the scoop on the left side, and the one on the right side can be seen beneath the Y in NAVY in the photo at left.

The little V-shaped device hanging beneath the aircraft is a cable guard called a standoff. It's purpose is to keep the ALE-50 towed decoy cable from fouling in the hook and horizontal tail. Some early Super Hornets were delivered without this device installed.

The arresting hook is mounted on a fairing between the engines. It extends just beyond the engine nozzles when it is in the retracted position. The tail hooks on some Super Hornets have the warning stripes painted on them, but the one on this F/A-18E does not.

EXTERIOR LIGHTING

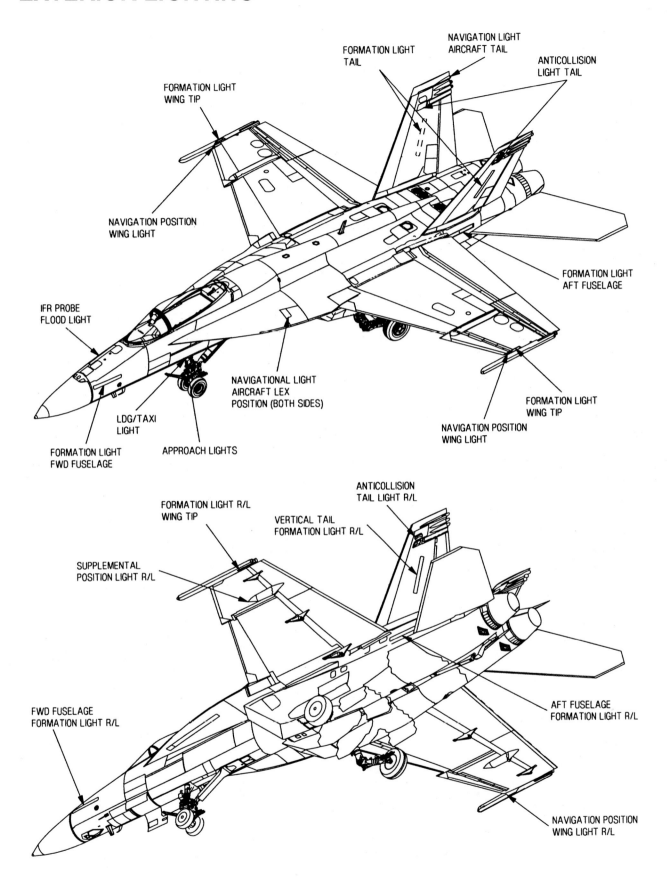

FORMATION LIGHT
TAIL

NAVIGATION LIGHT
AIRCRAFT TAIL

ANTICOLLISION
LIGHT TAIL

FORMATION LIGHT
WING TIP

NAVIGATION POSITION
WING LIGHT

FORMATION LIGHT
AFT FUSELAGE

IFR PROBE
FLOOD LIGHT

FORMATION LIGHT
WING TIP

NAVIGATIONAL LIGHT
AIRCRAFT LEX
POSITION (BOTH SIDES)

NAVIGATION POSITION
WING LIGHT

LDG/TAXI
LIGHT

FORMATION LIGHT
FWD FUSELAGE

APPROACH LIGHTS

ANTICOLLISION
TAIL LIGHT R/L

FORMATION LIGHT R/L
WING TIP

VERTICAL TAIL
FORMATION LIGHT R/L

SUPPLEMENTAL
POSITION LIGHT R/L

AFT FUSELAGE
FORMATION LIGHT R/L

FWD FUSELAGE
FORMATION LIGHT R/L

NAVIGATION POSITION
WING LIGHT R/L

The locations of exterior lights are shown in these drawings from the F/A-18E & F NATOPS manual. (U. S. Navy)

61

WING DETAILS

When the Hornet was originally designed, there was a saw tooth on the leading edge of the wing at the fold point. This was subsequently removed on production

Hornets to reduce drag, but the saw tooth has reappeared on Super Hornets. Flaps extend across the entire span of the leading edge. (Boeing)

Center left and right: Two small navigation position wing lights are on the leading edge of each fairing to which the wing tip launch rails are attached. The lights on the left wing are red, and those on the right wing are green.

Left: Wing tip formation light panels are mounted above and below the center of each launch rail. Like the light panels on the fuselage and tail, these appear to be a light yellow in color, but when they are turned on, they glow bright green.

A small navigation light is located on top of each LEX. The light on the left LEX, as shown in this view, is red, and the one on top of the right LEX is green. The screen covers the exhaust for the Liquid Cooling System.

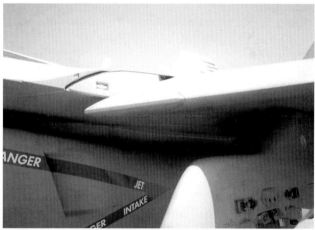

A dark gray non-slip area is applied to the top of the left LEX directly above the boarding ladder to make it safer for the aircrew to climb into or out of the cockpit. Also note the pull-out hand hold.

A close-up shows the inboard end of the leading edge flap on the left wing. When the aircraft is on the ground and the power is shut down, the leading edge flaps usually drop to this position.

In this view, the leading edge flaps are in their fully lowered position. Notice how the shape of the pylons provides clearance for the flaps.

The outer wing panels fold ninety degrees to conserve space on aircraft carriers. The leading edge flaps can be fully lowered even with the wings in the folded position.

A rear view of an F/A-18F provides a good look at the wings in the folded position. Note the small fairings in the vertical position just inboard of the folded outer pan-els. When the wings are extended, these porous fairings drop down horizontally and cover the wing fold hinge. (U. S. Navy)

During development, the Super Hornet experienced wing droop problems at the hinge. To correct this, porous fairings were developed which corrected the problem. The photo at left shows an earlier design of the porous fairing, while the one at right is more like the design used on production aircraft. (Boeing photos)

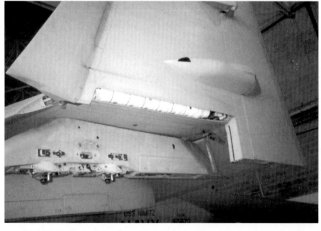

Details of the wing fold hinges are shown in these two views. The hinges are a simple rugged design and lack the complex arrangement of braces and actuators seen on some other types of aircraft. Note how the trailing section of the outer panel, including the aileron, angles down aft of the wing fold hinge.

Flaps cover the almost the full span of the inboard wing sections, while ailerons span a little more than the width of the outer or folding wing sections.

As on legacy Hornets, the ailerons can operate as standard ailerons or they can both be lowered to serve as flaps as shown in this photo and the one to the left.

The hinges for the right aileron are shown here beneath the wing. Note that the inboard hinge is part of a large faring which has a supplemental position light near its forward end. The lower formation light panel on the right wing tip is also visible.

The pylons have tapered trailing edges to allow movement of the flaps and ailerons. This photograph also shows the small hydraulic gage on the side of the fuselage below the flap. See the top right photo on page 60 for a close-up of this gage.

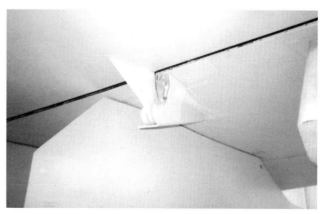

Each flap pivots on two hinges. This is the inboard hinge for the left flap. The inboard hinge for the right flap is identical.

The outboard hinge on each flap is located between the inboard and center wing pylons. This is the outboard hinge for the right flap.

TAIL DETAILS

The two vertical tails on the F/A-18E and F/A-18F are very much like those used on earlier Hornets, but detail differences do exist. Note the anti-collision light high on the tail. Below it is the air inlet for the vent tank located inside the tail.

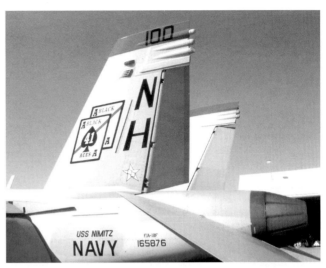

A formation light panel is on the outboard side of each vertical tail. The light panel can be seen between VFA-41's Ace of Spades insignia and the NH tail code. The three rudder hinges are also clearly visible in this view, because the rudders are turned to the right.

There are three antenna fairings at the top of the left vertical tail. From top to bottom, they contain the ALQ-165 Airborne Self-Protection Jammer's (ASPJ) high band transmit antenna, the ALQ-165 low band transmit antenna, and the ALR-67 aft receive antenna. The fuel jettison vent is just above the radar.

A white navigation light is at the aft end of the top fairing on the right vertical tail. Below the light is the fairing for the ALQ-165 aft low/high band receiving antenna, and below that is the ALR-67 receiving antenna. The fuel vent outlet is just above the rudder, and forward of it are the anti-collision light and the inlet for the fuel vent tank.

Details on the inboard surface of the right rudder, including the top and middle hinges, are visible in this close-up. There are no trim tabs on the rudders on any other control surface on the Super Hornet. Instead, the entire control surface is moved slightly as needed to establish proper trim.

The horizontal tail surfaces are an all-flying design, meaning the entire surface moves around a single pivot point near the center of the root chord.

The horizontal tails move together for pitch control and in opposite directions to provide roll control in conjunction with the ailerons.

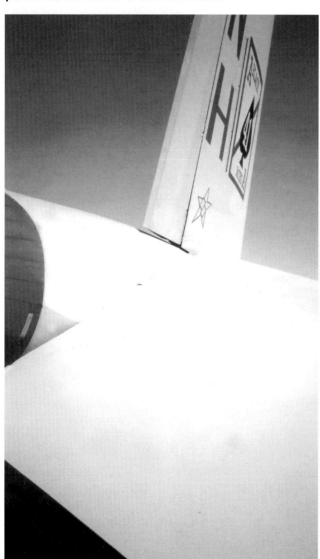

A walkway is outlined on the top of each horizontal tail surface at the root. NO STEP markings indicate where maintenance crewmen should not step on the surface.

When a Super Hornet is parked after a flight, the horizontal tails are in a neutral position just after the engines are shut down.

After the power has been off for a while, the horizontal tails drop to this position. They usually remain at this angle until power is reapplied.

STATIONS FOR EXTERNAL STORES

STATIONS 1 & 11

The Super Hornet was designed to carry a greater weapons load than earlier Hornets. External stores can be carried on eleven stations, two more than the previous variants. The stations are numbered 1 through 11, starting with the left wing tip and moving to the right wing tip. Stations 1 and 11 are the two wing tip stations, and they are primarily used as launch rails for AIM-9 Sidewinder air-to-air missiles.

An AIM-9M sidewinder is loaded on Station 11. During training, telemetry pods can also be carried on stations 1 and 11, and for weapons separations tests, pods with cameras are installed.

A rear view of the launch rail on station 11 shows its cross section. Note how the edge of the aileron is right next to the launch rail. The rail itself is attached only to the fixed part of the wing.

A rear quarter view shows that the tail of the AIM-9M does not come all the way back to the end of the launch rail when it is installed. Instead, it is approximately even with the trailing edge of the fixed portion of the wing.

The AIM-9M will soon be replaced with the AIM-9X and its expanded capability to engage targets at wider angles to the aircraft. This AIM-9X was on display at Andrews Air Force Base. (Rotramel)

STATIONS 2 & 10

Stations 2 and 10 are the outboard wing pylons. All six wing pylons are angled out four degrees at the front, but the two outboard pylons are also canted 3.5 degrees outward at the bottom as seen in this front view of Station 10. (Boeing)

An outside view of Station 10 shows the tapered shape of the SUU-80A pylon. The tapering provides clearance for the leading edge flaps and the aileron.

An underside view of the pylon on Station 10 shows the attachment points, ejector pins, and anti-sway braces. Note the pylon's close proximity to the wing fold.

Station 2 is the outboard wing station under the left wing. In this photo, as well as the one directly above, note how the pylon does not fit flush to the bottom of the wing. Instead, there is a considerable gap between the pylon and the wing, particularly at the aft end. All six wing pylons usually have the BRU-32 bomb rack installed, but at times other equipment is installed.

While most external stores, including free-fall and guided bombs, cluster bombs, and fuel tanks, are attached directly to the pylons, missiles, which are fired rather than dropped, require the use of launch rails which are attached to the pylons. This is an LAU-127A/A launch rail used for carrying a single AIM-120 AMRAAM air-to-air missile on this station.

STATIONS 3 & 9

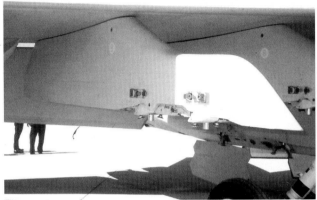

Stations 3 and 9 are the center stations under each wing. SUU-79/A pylons are carried on these stations, and although they look like the pylons used on earlier Hornets, they are different. This is the pylon on Station 9 under the right wing.

An outside front view shows the SUU-79/A pylon on Station 3 under the left wing. These pylons are wet, meaning that they can be used for external fuel tanks.

The pylons on Stations 3 and 9 are angled outward four degrees at the front, but unlike the pylons on Stations 2 and 10, they are not canted at an angle.

Ordnancemen load a GBU-16 laser guided bomb (LGB) on Station 3 beneath the left wing of an F/A-18E assigned to VFA-115. This action took place on the flight deck of USS ABRAHAM LINCOLN, CVN-72, on April 3, 2003, in preparation for a mission in support of Operation Iraqi Freedom. The crewmen are using a gas-powered Single Hoist Ordnance Loading System (SHOLS) to lift the weapon from its transporter up to the pylon. This device installs into a fitting on the side of the pylon between the two attachment lugs. The largest and heaviest stores carried on Stations 3 and 8 are the 480-gallon fuel tanks, and when full, these weigh approximately 3,000 pounds. (U. S. Navy)

STATIONS 4 & 8

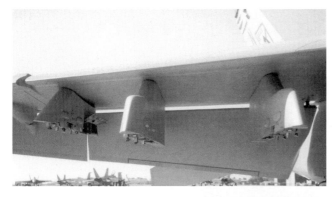

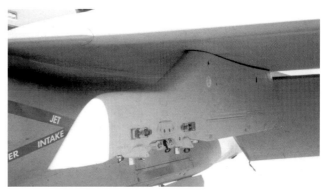

Above left: Stations 4 and 8 are the two wing stations closest to the fuselage. They carry the same SUU-79/A pylons as used on Stations 3 and 9. This front view shows the spacing between the three wing stations.

Above right: This is the pylon on Station 4. The pylons on Stations 4 and 8 are angled outward four degrees at the nose, but they are not canted at an angle to the wing.

Left: FPU-11 external fuel tanks are often carried on Stations 4 and 8. The fuel tanks used on Super Hornets are larger than those carried by the earlier versions of the Hornet. Each has a capacity of 480 gallons, and as many as five tanks can be carried at one time. Here, an external tank is loaded on Station 8.

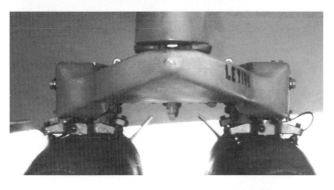

Center left: A front view shows the original Vertical Ejector Rack (VER) used on legacy Hornets to permit two weapons to be carried on a single pylon. (Rotramel)

Center right: The original VER was replaced by the Canted Vertical Ejector Rack (CVER), and this is now used on all Hornet variants. The CVER is wider than the VER, and each mount is angled outward 5.5 degrees for a total of 11 degrees. This provides better separation for the weapons when they are released. (Rotramel)

Right: Mk 82 500-pound bombs are loaded on CVERS attached to the pylons under the right wing of an F/A-18E. (U. S. Navy)

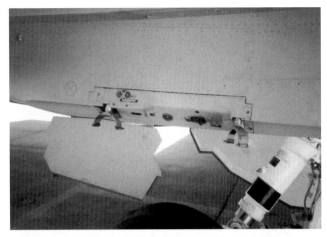

Stations 5 and 7 are known as the "cheek" stations, and they are on the lower edges of the center fuselage just outboard of the landing gear. This is Station 7 on the right side of the fuselage.

Station 5 is on the left side of the fuselage. The C-shaped brackets are part of the mounting equipment for AIM-7 Sparrow or AIM-120 AMRAAMs. The concave area in the fuselage conforms to the missile's body.

This rear quarter view shows how an AIM-120 AMRAAM fits into the concave area of the fuselage and the two C-shaped brackets. The AMRAAM is the store most often carried on Station 7.

This live AMRAAM was photographed on an F/A-18E at Lemoore just prior to a firing exercise. Super Hornets can also carry AIM-7 Sparrow radar-guided air-to-air missiles on Stations 5 and 7.

The most common and important store carried on Station 5 is the AN/ASQ-228(V)2 Advanced Targeting Forward Looking Infrared (ATFLIR) pod. This permits the Super Hornet to employ precision guided weapons, and it replaces the older AN/AAS-46 TFLIR pod. An identifying feature of the ATFLIR is the small aperture in the front of the pod's fairing for the Navigation FLIR (NAVFLIR). This aperture can be seen in this photo. The big advantage of the new NAVFLIR is that it is located inside the ATFLIR's fairing rather than being a separate pod system which requires the use of Station 7. This was the case with the old AN/AAR-55 NAVFLIR pod. (U. S. Navy)

STATION 6

Station 6 is the centerline station mounted beneath the fuselage of the aircraft. It is shown here with a D704 aerial refueling store installed. The aerial refueling store can only be carried on the centerline station. (Boeing)

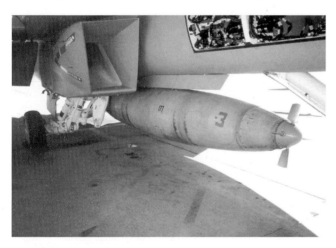

Center left and right: These two close-ups not only show the D704 aerial refueling store, but they also provide a good look at the SUU-78 pylon between the store and the fuselage. Note the angled leading edge of the pylon. Super Hornets often carry an aerial refueling store on the centerline, because they are now the Navy's primary carrier-borne tanker aircraft. When serving as tankers, Super Hornets will typically carry the aerial refueling store on the centerline station and two or four 480-gallon fuel tanks on Stations 3, 4, 8, and 9. Note the four blades of the power generator on the front of the store. (Left, Kinzey; right, Boeing)

Right: The most common store carried on Station 6 is an FPU-11 480-gallon external fuel tank.

SHARP

Above: The Super Hornet will not only serve as a fighter, attack aircraft, and aerial tanker. It will also be a reconnaissance aircraft using the new Shared Reconnaissance Pod (SHARP). This pod replaces the Tactical Air Reconnaissance Pod System (TARPS) used on some F-14 Tomcats. The initial delivery of the first SHARP Low-Rate Initial Production (LRIP) System from Raytheon took place on April 2, 2003. The Navy wasted no time getting the pod to the fleet, sending it to VFA-41 aboard USS NIMITZ, CVN-68. The pod is shown here on the centerline station of one of VFA-41's F/A-18Fs. (U. S. Navy)

Right: The same Super Hornet shown in the photo above is readied for launch with the SHARP pod on the centerline. (U. S. Navy)

The SHARP system is moved across the hangar deck aboard NIMITZ as VFA-41 personnel receive training on how to use the new system. (U. S. Navy)

Crewmen prepare the electro-optical and infrared equipment inside the pod's rotating mid-section prior to a mission over Iraq. (U. S. Navy)

EJECTION SEAT DETAILS

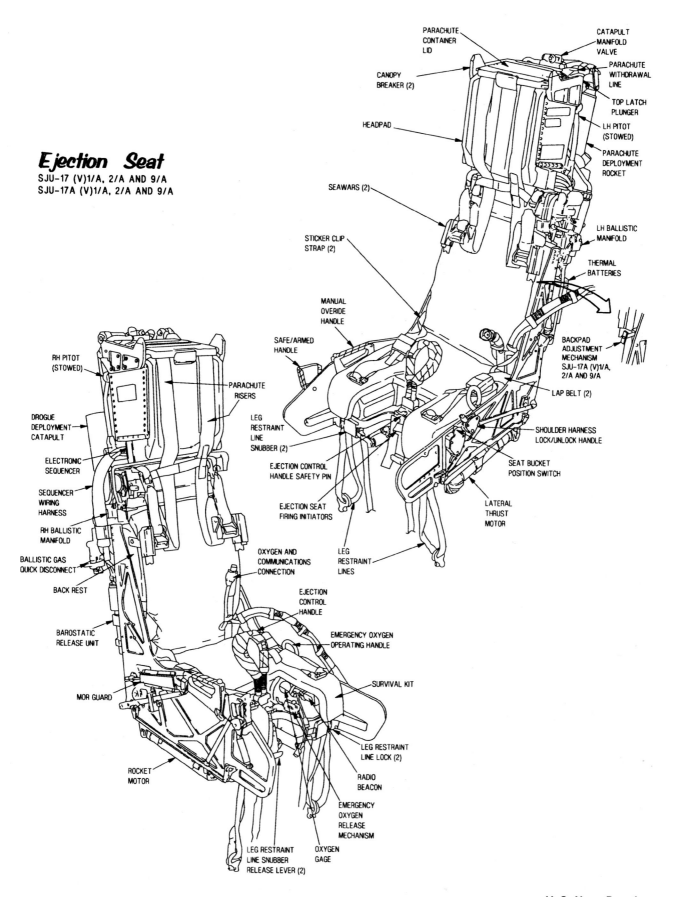

Ejection Seat
SJU-17 (V)1/A, 2/A AND 9/A
SJU-17A (V)1/A, 2/A AND 9/A

PARACHUTE CONTAINER LID

CATAPULT MANIFOLD VALVE

CANOPY BREAKER (2)

PARACHUTE WITHDRAWAL LINE

HEADPAD

TOP LATCH PLUNGER

LH PITOT (STOWED)

PARACHUTE DEPLOYMENT ROCKET

SEAWARS (2)

LH BALLISTIC MANIFOLD

STICKER CLIP STRAP (2)

THERMAL BATTERIES

MANUAL OVERIDE HANDLE

BACKPAD ADJUSTMENT MECHANISM SJU-17A (V)1/A, 2/A AND 9/A

SAFE/ARMED HANDLE

LAP BELT (2)

RH PITOT (STOWED)

PARACHUTE RISERS

DROGUE DEPLOYMENT CATAPULT

LEG RESTRAINT LINE SNUBBER (2)

SHOULDER HARNESS LOCK/UNLOCK HANDLE

ELECTRONIC SEQUENCER

EJECTION CONTROL HANDLE SAFETY PIN

SEAT BUCKET POSITION SWITCH

SEQUENCER WIRING HARNESS

EJECTION SEAT FIRING INITIATORS

LATERAL THRUST MOTOR

RH BALLISTIC MANIFOLD

OXYGEN AND COMMUNICATIONS CONNECTION

LEG RESTRAINT LINES

BALLISTIC GAS QUICK DISCONNECT

BACK REST

EJECTION CONTROL HANDLE

BAROSTATIC RELEASE UNIT

EMERGENCY OXYGEN OPERATING HANDLE

SURVIVAL KIT

MOR GUARD

LEG RESTRAINT LINE LOCK (2)

ROCKET MOTOR

RADIO BEACON

EMERGENCY OXYGEN RELEASE MECHANISM

LEG RESTRAINT LINE SNUBBER RELEASE LEVER (2)

OXYGEN GAGE

MODELERS SECTION

Note: Each volume in the Detail & Scale Series of aviation publications has a Modelers Summary in the back of the book. The Modelers Summary discusses the injection molded plastic model kits of the aircraft covered by the book, and all common modeling scales from 1/144th through 1/24th scale will be included. Highlights of the better kits in each scale will be discussed, and recommendations will be made with respect to which kit or kits in each scale are the best for the serious scale modeler to use. Once a kit has been purchased, the modeler should compare the various features of the kit to the detailed photographs in the book to determine how accurately and extensively they are represented. He can then decide what, if any, correcting and detailing work he wants to do to enhance the appearance of his model.

General Comments

Model manufacturers have often tried to be the first to produce a kit of a new aircraft, but in several cases, this has wound up being a disadvantage that has proven expensive for them. A good example is when several manufacturers released kits as soon as the first F-15 Eagle began flight testing. But their models represented that aircraft only, and by the time operational squadrons were flying F-15As, several noticeable changes had been made. These included reshaped wing tips and a redesigned speedbrake on the top of the aircraft. Changes were also made to the vertical tails. The sales of the early kits fell off dramatically when subsequent releases by other companies more accurately represented operational F-15s. As a result, the model manufacturers that had released the early kits were faced with expensive retooling costs, and some had to produce new kits.

Experiences like this, along with other changes in the marketing strategies of the few remaining model companies, has caused manufacturers to be more cautious when it comes to tooling and producing kits of new aircraft. Although the Super Hornet first flew in 1995, very few models have been released of the aircraft in spite of its importance in Naval Aviation. Those that have been produced suffer from

The Italeri 1/72nd scale F/A-18E represents an early production aircraft and has a number of noticeable inaccuracies. Bob Bartolacci used the Italeri kit to build this model of the CAG aircraft from VFA-115. (Bartolacci)

obvious inaccuracies and do not have the features added to production aircraft now used in operational squadrons.

As of early 2004, no model kits of the Super Hornet have been released in 1/144th scale or 1/32nd scale. Considering the prominent role the aircraft has, its increasing numbers, and its appealing appearance, it is certain that kits in these popular scales will be developed and released in the future. As this is written, new kits, which accurately represent production aircraft, are finally being issued in 1/72nd scale, and new 1/48th scale kits will be on the market before the end of 2004. Still more model kits of the F/A-18E and F/A-18F will certainly be released as the Super Hornet becomes the most numerous aircraft aboard the Navy's aircraft carriers.

1/72nd Scale Kits

Italeri F/A-18E

The first kits of the Super Hornet to be released were from Italeri. They appeared on the market in 1997, and they represented the first EMD aircraft. Markings in the kit were for E1 as illustrated at the bottom of page 8 of this book. Production features, including the "pizza box" on top of the nose and the standoff cable guard beneath the aft fuselage, are missing. The blade antenna on the spine is located too far forward. The real thing has never been that far forward, even on the EMD Super Hornets. The inner and center wing pylons represent those used on earlier versions of the Hornet rather than the SUU-79s used on the Super Hornets.

Perhaps the most inaccurate item on all of the Italeri models in both 1/72nd and 1/48th scales is that they have the large speedbrake located between the two vertical tails, and this can be displayed in both the opened or closed positions. This speedbrake was on the four earlier versions of the Hornet, but they are not on the Super Hornets. They

In November 2003, Hasegawa released a 1/72nd scale model of the F/A-18F. It is far superior in accuracy and detailing than the Italeri kit, and it is much more up to date with respect to the features found on production Super Hornets. (HobbyLink Japan)

must be assembled in the closed position, and the seams around them need to be filled and sanded.

Cockpit detail is sparse. The side consoles are too high above the seat, and detailing on the consoles and the instrument panel is provided by decals. The canopy can be assembled in the opened or closed positions, but the detailing behind the seat is lacking. The landing gear detail is better, and while the detailing inside the wells is not entirely accurate, it is quite acceptable for a 1/72nd scale model.

External stores include an external fuel tank for the centerline station, one AIM-120 AMRAAM for the right cheek station, and a FLIR pod for the left cheek station. AIM-9M Sidewinders are provided for the wing tip stations, and AGM-88 HARM, AGM-84 Harpoon, and AGM-84A-1C SLAM Enhanced Response (ER) missiles are included to go on the underwing pylons. The pylons are mounted parallel to the centerline rather than being angled four degrees outward, but this is because the kit was developed before this change was made to the real aircraft.

Although the kit is generally accurate in its overall shape and size, it lacks detailing and a number of the features of production aircraft. With the newer, better, and more up-to-date Hasegawa kits now coming out, we cannot recommend the Italeri models.

Italeri F/A-18F

Italeri's 1/72nd scale F/A-18F is basically the same kit as the F/A-18E reviewed above. A different cockpit tub, second seat, a different canopy, and a few other different parts are provided to build the two-seat version of the Super Hornet. The kit also features a slightly different ordnance load with the SLAM/ER missiles being replaced by a second pair of Harpoons. The FLIR pod is not included, but a second AMRAAM is provided to go on the left cheek station. Otherwise all of the features in this kit are the same as in the F/A-18E kit. Decals are provided for F1 as it appeared early in the test flight program. Again, with the new Hasegawa F/A-18F available in 1/72nd scale, we cannot recommend the Italeri kit.

Hasegawa F/A-18F

Hasegawa released the first of its 1/72nd scale Super Hornet models just as this book was being completed. Thanks to HobbyLink Japan, a review sample was obtained in time to be included here.

The model represents a production F/A-18F with all of the appropriate features including the "pizza box" on top of the nose and the standoff cable guard under the aft fuselage. The wing pylons are angled outward at the proper four-degree angle, but be sure to assemble the outboard wing pylons with the three and one-half degree cant as shown in the top left photo on page 69.

Surface scribing is recessed and generally accurate, however the screen for the Liquid Cooling System's heat exchanger is missing from the top of the left LEX. An interesting note is that the boundary layer holes inside the inlets, the chaff/flare dispensers under the inlets, and gun gas vents beneath the nose are represented by decals rather than being engraved into the plastic.

Cockpit detailing includes a tub, two ejection seats,

Joe Hegedus made numerous corrections and additions to the 1/48th scale Italeri F/A-18E to build this model of an early Super Hornet assigned to the Strike Test program at NAS Patuxent River, Maryland. The aircraft was used in weapons separation tests. (Hegedus)

instrument panels, a control column, and coamings to go above the instrument panels. The proportions of the tub and the height of the consoles are more accurate than in the Italeri 1/72nd scale kits, but decals provide the detailing on the instrument panels and consoles. The windscreen and canopy are clear and thin, but the detailing behind the rear seat is lacking. The actuating mechanism and link are much better represented than in the Italeri kits, and the canopy can be assembled in the opened or closed positions.

Hasegawa included AIM-9X Sidewinder missiles for the wing tips and two AIM-120 AMRAAMs are provided to go on launch rails beneath Stations 2 and 10. CVERs go on Stations 3 and 9, but no weapons are included for them. These CVERs are wider than the VERs that Hasegawa used in their previous Hornet kits, and this is correct, but the mounting brackets are not canted 5.5 degrees outward as they should be. This is easily fixed with a file, and the modeler can chose appropriate weapons for the CVERs from various armament kits that are available separately. It would have been nice if Hasegawa had provided some JDAMs for this kit, because these new weapons are not presently available in weapons sets or many other kits.

Other external stores include three external fuel tanks for Stations 4, 6, and 8. An old AN/AAS-38 FLIR pod is provided for the left cheek station, and this is disappointing, because the Super Hornet will use the more advanced AN/ASQ-228(V)2 ATFLIR pod which is not currently available in other kits. Perhaps an after-market company will correct this problem. Super Hornets will almost always fly with the ATFLIR pod for ground attack missions.

Decals are provided for the CAG aircraft of VFA-2 with similar markings to the squadron commander's aircraft shown in the lower photograph on page 37. Optional markings are provided for an aircraft from VFA-102. These are shown in the top photograph on page 37. Both NG and NF tail codes are included for this aircraft. It is understandable

that Hasegawa chose these markings, because VFA-102 has deployed to Japan as the first Super Hornet squadron to be forward deployed outside the United States.

Overall this is an excellent kit, and it is far superior to the Italeri F/A-18F. It is engineered so that it can also be released as an F/A-18E, and this is sure to happen, because one of the parts trees has "F/A-18E/F" engraved on it. We highly recommend this kit and look forward to the release of the F/A-18E version.

Review sample courtesy of HobbyLink Japan

1/48th Scale Kits

Italeri F/A-18E

Italeri's 1/48th scale model was the first Super Hornet kit available in this scale. It has also been released under the Revell-Germany label with different decals. The model is reasonably accurate in size and shape, with the possible exception of the canopy which appears to be a bit flat. But the kit has numerous shortcomings in details, and it represents an LRIP I aircraft. Further, the fit is poor for most of the assemblies, so a considerable amount of filler is required on almost all of the seams. Panel detail is of the recessed type, so replacing it is easier after all the required body work.

As with their 1/72nd scale kits, Italeri included the speedbrake between the vertical fins, but these were only on the FA-18A/B/C/D. This feature is not on the Super Hornets.

The engine intakes are odd, being quite shallow in depth with a strange shape to match up with the engine compressor faces which are too small.

The cockpit is very poor, with no detailing on the instrument panel or side consoles. Instead, decals are provided for these areas. This may be acceptable for 1/72nd scale models, but some raised detailing is desirable on 1/48th scale kits. The seat is fair, and it can be used if some detailing is accomplished to add belts and other features.

The LEX vents, located inboard of the inner wing's leading edge flaps, may be assembled in either the raised or lowered positions, but the real ones are locked closed. The fit of these is poor, as is the fit of the LEX spoilers forward of the

Stan Parker used markings for VFA-41 on Italeri's 1/48th scale F/A-18F. Like their 1/72nd scale kits, Italeri's 1/48th scale Super Hornets have a number of serious inaccuracies and represent early production aircraft. (Parker)

vents. The spoilers can also be assembled in the opened or closed position, but they are almost never seen open on the ground.

The wing pylons are representative of the SUU-63 pylons used on the earlier Hornet versions. The SUU-79, used on the Super Hornet, is longer with a tapered fairing on the rear. SUU-79 pylons also incorporate fairings around the anti-sway braces on the bomb racks which the SUU-63 lacks. The centerline pylon is also incorrect. The kit has the early SUU-62 pylon with vertical leading and trailing edges used on legacy Hornets, while the SUU-78 used on the F/A-18E and F/A-18F has angled leading and trailing edges like the later lot of centerline pylons used on the earlier variants. The kit's outboard SUU-80 pylons are acceptable, but there are holes for the mounting pegs on the LAU-118 HARM launch rails that need to be filled if the rails are not used.

The orientation of the wing pylons is incorrect, being parallel to the centerline rather than being angled outward four degrees at the leading edge. Likewise, the outboard pylons are not canted away from the airplane 3.5 degrees.

The pizza box on the upper nose is missing. In all fairness, the decals provided are for an LRIP-I Super Hornet which was delivered without this equipment installed. The pizza box was not added until LRIP-II, so a Super Hornet with a Bureau Number of 165660 or higher should have it. Aircraft with Bureau Numbers lower than that were not built with this feature, but it was retrofitted to some of them.

There is an adapter included to fit a FLIR pod on the left intake station, but the parts included are inaccurate. The parts are for the laser spot tracking/strike camera pod, but this pod is not carried on the left intake; and it is not used on the Super Hornet. It was only carried on the right intake of legacy Hornets.

A variety of underwing stores are provided including an AIM-120 for the right cheek station, a pair of passable HARM and Harpoon missiles for the underwing pylons, and two poor GBU-12 laser guided bombs that should not be used.

There are also a pair of AIM-9M Sidewinders for the wing tips that are useable but are a bit undersized. A fuel tank is included for the centerline, but it is more representative of the FPU-8 330-gallon tank used on the legacy Hornets than the FPU-11 480-gallon tank used on the F/A-18E and F/A-18F. The 330-gallon tank isn't used on the Super Hornet.

The kit decals are for an LRIP-I F/A-18E assigned to the Fleet Replenishment Squadron, VFA-122. Overall, this is not a very good kit, and much correcting and detailing is required to build an accurate representation of a production F/A-18E. With the Revell-Monogram Super Hornet kits scheduled for release in 2004, we recommend waiting for them to become available.

Italeri F/A-18F

This kit is basically the same as the F/A-18E reviewed immediately above. Parts are provided for the second cockpit and the longer canopy is included. The FLIR pod is replaced with another AIM-120 AMRAAM missile. Decals are for an F/A-18F from VFA-122. Again, we recommend waiting for the Revell-Monogram releases which are certain to be more accurate and up-to-date than this kit from Italeri.

Revell-Monogram F/A-18E and F/A-18F

Revell-Monogram has announced the release of an F/A-18E Super Hornet in 1/48th scale for the summer of 2004. At press time for this book, the first test shot was not available, but Detail & Scale was involved in the research and planning for this kit, so some comments can be made here.

The kit is engineered so it can be released as both an F/A-18E and F/A-18F, so the two seat version will certainly follow the initial release of the F/A-18E. The models will represent a production aircraft complete with the "pizza box" on the nose and the standoff beneath the rear fuselage. The wing pylons will be mounted at the proper angles. The initial release will include markings for the CAG and squadron commander's aircraft of VFA-14 at NAS Lemoore, California. These are also the markings used by the squadron during its deployment aboard USS NIMITZ, CVN-68, in support of Operation Iraqi Freedom. These 1/48th scale Super Hornet kits promise to be more accurate, have better detailing, and be more up-to-date than the Italeri kits.

More Machines and Men from squadron/signal publications

Aircraft in Action

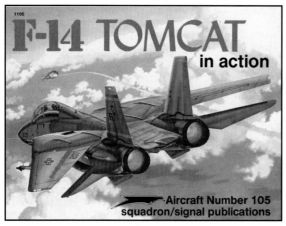

1105 F-14 Tomcat

Armor in Action

2026 M1 Abrams

Walk Around

5518 F/A-18 Hornet

Combat Troops in Action

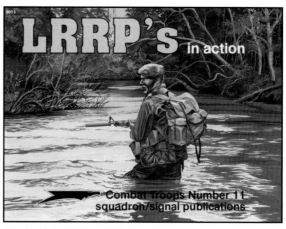

3011 LLRP's, Pt. 1

Warships in Action

4002 US Subs

Detail & Scale

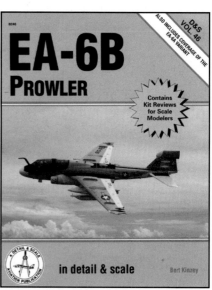

8246 EA-6B Prowler

For a complete listing of squadron/signal books, go to www.squadron.com